PLAYDHD

Permission To Play...
A Prescription For Adults With ADHD

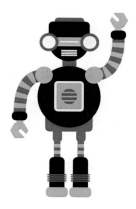

By

Kirsten Milliken PH.D., PCC
PSYCHOLOGIST and ADHD COACH

Design and Illustration By
Morgan Pickard
HOWLER MONKEY DESIGN STUDIO

DISCLAIMER:

Warning: This book may cause you to play more. The consequences of this can include enjoying work, looking forward to coming home, dealing effectively with challenges and being happy.

This book is intended for people with ADHD (diagnosed, undiagnosed or self-diagnosed), with attention problems, as well as for those who are just curious about the benefits of play.

Neither the publisher nor the author are engaged in rendering professional advice or services to the individual reader. The ideas, procedures, and suggestions in this book are not intended as a substitute for consulting with a coach, mental health or medical professional. All matters regarding health require supervision by a licensed professional. Neither the authors nor the publisher shall be liable or responsible for any loss or damage allegedly arising from any information or suggestions in this book.

While the author has made every effort to provide accurate Internet addresses at the time of publication, neither the publisher no the authors assume any responsibility for errors, or for changes that occur after publication. Further, the publisher does not have any control over and does not assume any responsibility for author or third-party websites or their content.

Any typos or misspellings are unintentional. I dictate messages to my pet squirrel who has dexterity issues.

ACKNOWLEDGEMENTS

This book was begun years ago, and, in true ADHD fashion, was revised, restarted, edited, and recreated many times thanks to the support, inspirations, suggestions, and love from my family and tribe of playmates. This includes, but is not limited to:

The best kids in the whole world, Oliver and Harris

My parents, Susan and Alan

My only sister, Tiffany

My fabulous uncle, Ken

All my ex-husbands and partners

Uber project manager Jeff Zupancic

Word wizard Amy Paradysz

An unexpected "find," Morgan Pickard

My mentor and friend and very "serious player," Jeff Copper

A role model for all the ways to play, Bernie DeKoven

Everyone who helped with the creation and content on PlayDHD. com

My entire ADHD tribe of professionals, clients, friends, and friends I've yet to meet

My network of neuro-typical friends and professionals

Everyone who ever published anything of any interest to me

There are many other "players" who helped along the way, both intentionally and unknowingly. Many people have shared their ideas, talked through the concept of play with me, helped me to organize my thoughts, and just played with me in general. Thank you! Let's play again soon!

CONTENTS

INTRODUCTION

YOU HAVE ADHD! This can sound like a life sentence to hell. (You have a disorder. A deficit of attention. There is something very WRONG with you.) When they give you the news, no one says "Welcome to the tribe!" No one focuses on all the cool things about having ADHD (and, trust me, there are some). If you—or someone you care about—just got the diagnosis of ADHD, you may have a million questions about what it means. Are there things you can do to help manage your symptoms? Is medication the only or best option for treatment? Are there other choices?

In short, yes. There are numerous options, including coaching, therapy, exercise, diet, neurofeedback, sleep management, supplements, and, of course, prescription medication that can effectively address the symptoms of ADHD. Medication is the "easiest" treatment in that it only requires a prescription, a daily reminder, and some water. Medications generally work in 20–30 minutes, last for a period of time, and then they don't, unless you take more.

Other forms of treatment, such as exercise, sleep, coaching, diet, take more effort and persistence to have an impact on symptoms of ADHD. In fact, they can be considered "work." Face it, if these methods were "convenient," fewer people might choose to take prescription medications. You wouldn't take even a tiny chance of becoming psychotic or dying because of an issue with medication if there was another easy way to manage ADHD that made you feel better immediately, would you? And, yes, some stimulant prescriptions list psychosis and death as potential side effects!

I'm here to tell you—[insert dramatic pause]—there is another option… PLAY!

You already know how to do this—or at least you did long ago. You can be playful almost anywhere anytime. You can be private about it or yell it out loud. The side effects of play are nothing to worry about;

productivity, creativity, laughter, and enjoyment. And who doesn't want to be around a playful person?

PlayDHD is about using the most effective non-medication intervention for managing ADHD—play!

It is my hope that this book will inspire you and give you some tools to start your own journey to reclaiming a playful approach to life and alleviating some of the challenges of ADHD that may be getting in your way.

About the Book

There are many other books that can guide you to develop better habits and routines when it comes to managing ADHD with diet, medication, sleep, and exercise. This book will not tell you what to eat, whether you should take medications, how to develop better sleep habits, or how fantastic exercise is for you. Though I will present some of the basics, you will not learn the detailed science and research about ADHD in this book. There is no "cure" for ADHD, so there won't be one in this book. Finally, if you're looking for how to catch fish, that won't be in here either.

If you are an adult with ADHD, this book is your prescription to play. Other experts in the field may tell you to take a pill, get more rest, exercise, train your brain, or whatever else it takes to manage impulsivity, inattention, poor time management, lack of motivation, memory struggles, and other symptoms related to ADHD. But they might not talk much about how fun and play can have a substantial effect on how you manage your ADHD symptoms.

ADHD is a serious problem. But your approach to it doesn't have to be serious. This book focuses on how developing a more playful mindset and habit of engaging in playful activities can actually help you to manage your ADHD. After a lifetime of being urged to stop goofing off and to take things more seriously, I'm telling you that play is what you need to do to better manage your difficulties with attention.

ADHD and Play—they're a perfect marriage. Play is the antidote to the challenges of ADHD: interest, attention, and motivation. Among people with ADHD, I find those who are playful while at work are happier and more productive. The same can be said of people with ADHD who are more playful in their relationships. People who travel, try new things, go on adventures, and just have fun have more successful relationships. Yes, this is true for everyone, not just for people with ADHD. But the impact is even more profound for those with ADHD.

As an adult there is a stigma about play. We're trained to take things seriously, work hard, and not "goof off." We are told to "grow up," and if we smile in a tense situation we are reminded, "This is serious." People with ADHD tend to feel even more pressure to be taken seriously. The words of adults repeating these mantras about the importance of being serious, working hard, and NOT playing so that we could "meet our potential" are lodged in our brains. It's likely that you were never encouraged to play to meet your potential, much less to have fun in an effort to be more creative, happy, energetic, and productive.

Enter Dr. Milliken—that's me—stage right (as in the side of the brain that likes to play), telling the ADHD audience to forget those old messages and start PLAYING MORE!

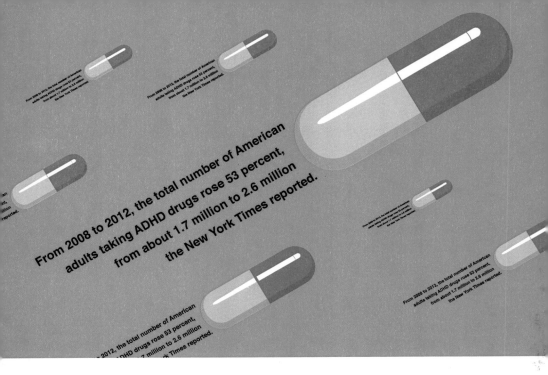

From 2008 to 2012, the total number of American adults taking ADHD drugs rose 53 percent, from about 1.7 million to 2.6 million the New York Times reported.

Who the Heck Is Dr. Milliken?

I'm a psychologist. You might not typically think a book by a psychologist is going to be a fun, light read. Likewise, most of my clients are surprised that when I offer them a seat in my office their options are a butterfly chair, a Move™ stool, a pile of beanbag chairs, or chairs on wheels. Looking around, they notice all of the "play stuff" in my office—a magic wand, stress balls, building materials, drawing tools, fidget toys, hula hoops, darts, a jump rope, a yo-yo, and games. "Do you work with kids?" they ask. Yes, I evaluate children. But most of my regular clients are adults.

I have always loved working with clients who have ADHD and other learning differences. I didn't always know why, but I found it easy to empathize with their experiences. In 2010 my son was diagnosed with ADHD. Ironically, it was only after this diagnosis that I asked, "Who did he get that from?" My ex-husband was kind enough to say, "You, of course! I just didn't know what it was called." Thanks, Harry!

Coming to the realization that I also had ADHD was a bit embarrassing. At the same time, it put a good number of difficulties and strengths I had throughout my life into perspective. Diagnostic labels are not my favorite part of psychology, but I found that having a diagnosis gave me a foundation to start understanding my unique brand of ADHD and to begin identifying strategies to improve my relationships, work habits, and life. I consider myself successful and well-respected as a psychologist. But I had always felt that something was holding me back from attaining a much higher level of success personally and professionally.

Within a year of my son's diagnosis I decided to pursue a long-term goal of becoming an ADHD coach. During this process I was tasked with identifying my own core values, and play came out at the top of my list. Right then and there I embarked on a quest to learn all I could about play and its connection to ADHD.

My "job" became paying attention to play every day—from what I read, to how I pay attention, and what catches my attention. Ordinary conversations became interesting exchanges of playful banter. I smiled at what other people thought of as "ordinary" or "boring" because I was paying attention to the playful aspects. At home and work I approach the painfully mundane tasks that I am required to do in a more playful manner. While there are still events that I struggle to "play" with, I do enjoy my life more because I am focused on living life paying attention through the lens of play. I feel more engaged with what I do, I am more thoughtful about how to enjoy even mundane tasks, and I make sure to have fun every day. I take my ADHD medications some days, but I "manage" my ADHD brain every day by triggering the neurochemicals it needs by playing.

Many of my clients are professionals and entrepreneurs with ADHD (or "undiagnosed" problems with attention) who are struggling in relationships and at work. They are "working hard" to try to keep up, meet deadlines, not disappoint anyone, and meet their potential. The harder they work the less time they have to relax, much less play. And while they are working harder, success can remain elusive. Partners, spouses, children, bosses, co-workers, and friends are seen as "demanding" or sources of guilt, and free time is merely a time to catch up on sleep. Their goal is to "be happy" or "have more balance" in their lives.

Since I made the personal connection, I have been incorporating play in my work with ADHD clients. Some take to it slowly, and others are all in from the start. Either way, it is an honor to watch the transformation they make from working harder to playing at work and in the rest of their life. This in turns leads to their success, happiness, and enjoyment of life. Rather than thinking of having "work-life balance" they are learning to incorporate a playful mindset into all aspects of their life.

My clients enjoy becoming reacquainted with their favorite ways to play and are happy to experiment with play to manage even their most challenging symptoms of ADHD. They join team sports, go with friends to comedy clubs, or re-ignite their artistic passions. They approach problems with a more playful attitude and find solutions that had eluded them when they were stuck in a more serious mindset. Most partners, parents, friends, and even bosses enjoy the "side effects" of my clients being more playful, happy, productive, and fun.

Who This Book Is For

This book is for adults who have ADHD—whether they have a confirmed diagnosis or not—as well as the important people in their lives who care about them.

In particular, this book is for those adults with ADHD who have "lost their mojo" at home and work. For those of you who used to be fun but now just work harder; who used to know how to make a boring day interesting and couldn't wait for days off to have adventures, and now have little free time and enjoy watching reality shows when they do; or who could come up with a million ways to do what everyone else had only two ways to do, and now would rather just go with one of the other people's two ideas.

If you loved your partner, your work, and your life but now wonder "what happened," this book is for you. Actually, it's for anyone who wants to be inspired to play more.

You might be afraid of not being taken seriously. You might be afraid to look silly. You might barely remember how to play. That's okay. Don't let fear stop you.

"Play is the joy of being fully present and engaged without fear of failure, a pleasant venture into the unknown."

—*Dana Keller,*
  researcher/writer/consultant and play advocate

Are You Ready to Play?

If all this talk about play has you on the verge of a panic attack, if you feel like you might suffocate, or the idea just feels too risky, you may have other "work" that you need to do before you are prepared to incorporate play into your success journey on a regular basis. This non-book can introduce you to the idea of play and being playful. By reading even parts of this non-book you can at least learn what you are saying "no" to. You will be surprised at how simple being more playful or engaging in play can be -- even if you only do it once in a while.

Here's a promise: Becoming more playful won't kill you. It won't make you psychotic. It won't cause hair loss or diarrhea (bonus, right?).

I have asked many people in the ADHD tribe for their thoughts about play. While most of them were excited to talk about it, many of them admitted to having some hesitancy about committing to using play as part of a way to manage their symptoms of ADHD. Perhaps some of what they asked me to include in a book about play and ADHD will resonate for you:

"Can you give me permission to play?"

"Can I actually use play to overcome procrastination?"

"I feel guilty when I play because it seems like it's just a way to procrastinate."

"Can play actually make me more productive?"

"Is there research that 'proves' play helps manage ADHD?"

Many of the requests were aimed at asking for a reputable authority to pit against the voices that tell us to "stop playing" and "get serious."

I can give permission. That's easy, and it might get you to change your behavior for a few days. But then you'll drift back into working harder to get ahead, forcing yourself to focus. When do you take a suggestion and stick with it? Do you listen to advice from your partner? Your parents? Your kids? Friends? Your doctor?

When your doctor says, "Take this medication," how often do you ignore his or her advice? If you are like me, not often. No, you go to the drugstore and get your medication and take it as prescribed. The rest of this book contains plenty of education on this innovative intervention. But here I'm going to cut to the chase and give you permission to get started playing and manage some of your symptoms of ADHD as soon as you feel inspired. I'm not only giving you permission, I'm giving you a PRESCRIPTION TO PLAY.

You can download a copy of this prescription by going to PlayDHD.com

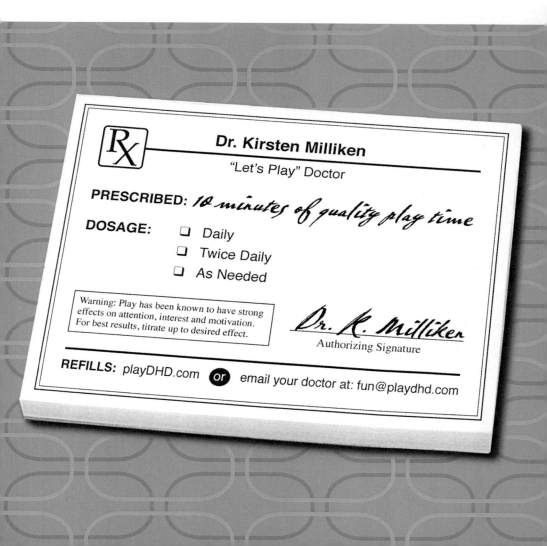

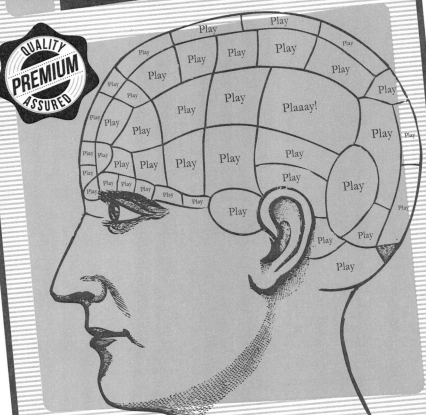

NEW

ADHD
BRAIN
ADVANCED CREATIVITY MODEL

QUALITY
PREMIUM
ASSURED

Play
Play
Play
Play
Play
Play
Play
Play
Play
Play
Play
Play
Play
Play
Play
Play
Play
Play
Play
Play
Plaaay!
Play
Play
Play
Play
Play
Play
Play
Play
Play
Play
Play
Play
Play
Play
Play
Play
Play
Play
Play
Play
Play

OWNER'S MANUAL

CHAPTER 1
ALL ABOUT ADHD

So, What Really Is ADHD?

Now that's you've got your prescription to play, and before we dive into the how-to of being playful, I want to tell you a bit about your fabulous ADHD brain and how play affects that brain. I want to give you a lay of the land—or, in this case, the playground. First let's clear up what ADHD is and what it isn't.

ADHD is not a personality flaw.

Having ADHD is not a weakness of character. Having ADHD does not mean you are lazy, stupid, or crazy (paraphrasing the ADHD self-help book by Kate Kelly and Peggy Ramundo, You Mean I'm Not Lazy, Stupid or Crazy?!)

ADHD is not something you can "cure."

ADHD is a difference in your brain. Unless you plan to get a lobotomy (please don't!) or a brain transplant (again, please don't!), this is how you are wired.

No two brains are the same. We all have differences. ADHD just happens to be a difference that has a diagnostic label. In a traditional school or work setting, having ADHD may make it challenging for you to sustain attention or sit still, hence the name "Attention Deficit Hyperactivity Disorder."

Ironically, people with ADHD can also have hyperfocus—or abundance of attention—when they are interested and motivated. As a clinician, I hear this all the time. "My kid can't have ADHD. He can focus on video games for hours at a time." Well, your kid likes video games!

Researchers have spent inordinate amounts of time and bazillions of dollars investigating the causes and effects of ADHD. Scientists have looked at images of the brain structures of people with and without ADHD. They have considered causes such as your mother smoking or drinking while pregnant, watching too much television (you, not your mother), being dropped on your head, eating foods with red dye (or pesticides or sugar), and plain old "bad" parenting. The consensus is that ADHD is caused by differences in your chemical, genetic, and physical (brain) makeup.

I have ADHD. I'm also a psychologist who has worked with hundreds of clients with ADHD. And I can tell you there is no one cause, no one treatment, no one way that ADHD presents itself, and no one sure-fire method for managing the challenges that come with ADHD.

We are complex human beings, each of us made up of interconnected neurological, chemical, unconscious, and conscious systems within ourselves. When we are challenged by an urge to procrastinate, struggling to pay attention, or trying to manage our excitement about a new endeavor, these feelings are caused by and have an effect on all of our systems in different ways, both within ourselves and in our lives. They can result in us being late for important appointments, make us doubt ourselves, cause us to overeat, disrupt our sleep, and cause conflicts in our relationships, to name a few. These same challenges in some situations also cause us to be passionate in our endeavors, creative and open to new ideas, and willing to take risks.

Taking the Mystery out of What's Happening in Your ADHD Brain

ADHD is all in your head -- I mean, it's in your brain! It is a difference in the structure and chemicals of your brain. Specifically, there are differences in your frontal cortex and dopamine system compared to someone who does not have ADHD. And if that more than satisfies your curiosity, feel free to skip ahead to a chapter you think will be more interesting (how very ADHD of you!). But I must warn you that someone is likely to ask how play helps manage the symptoms of ADHD, and you may want to have a more scientific explanation of how the ADHD brain works and how play activates it in a way that turns you into a superstar.

It's All Your Family's Fault!

Go ahead and blame your parents. ADHD has consistently been shown to be among the most heritable of all psychiatric conditions. If your kid has been diagnosed, you may (like me!) find yourself looking in the mirror wondering if you are the genetic link. A study conducted in 2012 at UCLA examined 256 parents of children with ADHD and found that 55% of these families had at least one parent affected by the disorder. A number of twin studies have found that the heritability of ADHD is about 76% in the population. So what have you inherited? Read on…

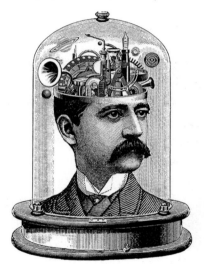

The Noggin

Let's start with the differences in the structure of the ADHD brain. To make it short and sweet, people with ADHD have less "stuff" in the frontal cortex. If you want to read the long version you can look it up online. You'll find phrases like "morphometric magnetic resonance imaging," "cortical thickness," "superior frontal and orbitofrontal cortex," "anterior cingulate cortex," and "temporoparietal, cerebellar, and occipital." So what the heck does that mean to you? In English and with an image:

The majority of this evidence suggests that a region known as the frontal cortex (the orange area in the picture below) is involved in ADHD.

Within the frontal cortex resides the prefrontal cortex, which takes up most of the area of the frontal cortex. It is the lobe that helps the brain sort through stimulation and decide what information is relevant and what to ignore. When the prefrontal cortex is operating optimally it takes in information, filters the options, uses good judgment, and strongly suggests the best choice and actions. It inhibits impulsive actions, focuses attention on what is important, and helps balance our desire for immediate gratification with good long-term outcomes.

It may be obvious to you at this point that if you have a difference in your prefrontal cortex you might get symptoms of ADHD.

Brain-imaging studies find that the prefrontal cortex of individuals with ADHD is smaller than that of individuals who do not have the disorder. Sometimes size does matter!

Transmission

In addition to the differences in structures of the brain, research also suggests that inappropriate levels of the chemicals that transmit nerve impulses throughout your brain (neurotransmitters) may also impair prefrontal cortex functions in people with ADHD. Play can play an important role in regulating these chemicals (yes, I used the word play twice in the sentence on purpose).

One of the neurotransmitters, dopamine, is often called the "feel good" brain chemical. During pleasurable experiences, dopamine is released into the synapses in your brain.

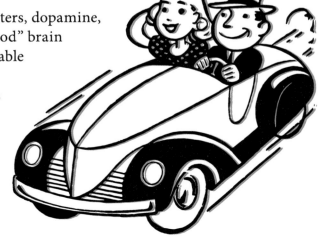

Depending on what research you pay attention to, symptoms of ADHD are related to problems resulting from:

a) Less dopamine
b) The transporter (sender) "sucks back" dopamine in the synapse prematurely (what I like to call "premature suckback")
c) The receptors that "catch" the dopamine on the other side of the synapse are inefficient.

There are a few ways to address these problems and ultimately increase dopamine transmission in the brain to a level of normal function. Those ways include stimulant medications, illicit substances (definitely not recommended!), and play. I'll let you guess which of these three has the fewest negative side effects.

Research has shown that there is a significant deficit in the function of the dopamine reward pathways in individuals who have ADHD. This translates into a decreased sensitivity to being engaged by activities that are not inherently rewarding or reinforcing. And this could explain the paradoxical perspective of many parents who say their kids can focus for hours playing video games but they can't focus at all at school. When the reward pathway is activated (say, by having fun), people with ADHD can pay attention for long periods of time. And that feels great! This concept also provides an explanation of why the stimulant medications used for ADHD actually make the task seem more rewarding or exciting. Stimulant medications increase levels of dopamine in our brains, thus increasing activity in the dopamine reward pathways. If you take one of these prescribed medications you might perceive otherwise boring tasks as much more interesting.

This is also the key to why play is another effective way to manage the symptoms of ADHD. When we are engaged in pleasurable activity more dopamine is released in our brain, combatting the low levels and premature suckback of dopamine in our synapses (I thought it would be fun to use the phrase "premature suckback" again).

There is a lot more to it. The details would might make your head swim. But this is enough to understand why you have ADHD and why play can help you.

If you have an ADHD brain, you likely have certain symptoms. When you are not in a playful mood, you are likely to notice more of these symptoms. The following sections talk about some of the symptoms used to diagnose ADHD, as well as some of the "other" symptoms that may be a manifestation of your ADHD as an adult.

What's in a Diagnosis?

I want to share the symptoms of ADHD so that you can have some idea of when yours is affecting you. You should not assume that every challenge or problem you have is related to ADHD. You want to pay attention to what symptoms and challenges are being caused by ADHD so you can know when you are managing them and what works to reduce their impact.

Symptoms (both formal symptoms and what the rest of us know to be true)

If you are being treated with medication or ever received disability accommodations in a school or work setting, you've probably had a "formal diagnosis" made by a qualified medical or mental health professional (like me!). As with any diagnosis, you have to meet certain criteria to be "officially" diagnosed (and to have your insurance pay the bill). ADHD is identified in the medical community as a "mental disorder." In diagnostic terms, the symptoms include problems in three broad areas: inattention, hyperactivity, and impulsivity. The reality of ADHD is that it affects self-management, mood, health, organization, relationships, work, education, success, and happiness. Argh!

The DSM-5 criteria for ADHD state that several symptoms must be present prior to age 12, that the symptoms occur across multiple settings, and that they impact academic, social or occupational functioning. It was not until 2014, with the release of the fifth edition of the Diagnostic and Statistical Manual (DSM-5), that the medical professional community formally acknowledged that symptoms of ADHD can persist into adulthood. With this, however, has come the concept of "Adult ADHD."

Here are the formal symptoms, excerpted from the Diagnostic and Statistical Manual. Realize that these symptoms are looked at across settings and in terms of how pervasive they are. Everyone has some of these symptoms sometimes; that doesn't mean they have ADHD.

THE DSM-5 CRITERIA FOR A DIAGNOSIS OF ADHD:

Inattentive presentation:

1. Fails to give close attention to details or makes careless mistakes.

    I never finish all the dishes in the sink.
2. Has difficulty sustaining attention.

    I want to talk to you about… oh, look, a squirrel!
3. Does not appear to listen.

    Sometimes it's more interesting to think about what happened last night.
4. Struggles to follow through on instructions.

    I can't remember more than two steps, then I get lost.
5. Has difficulty with organization.

Has anyone seen the really important document I swear was in this pile last week?
6. Avoids or dislikes tasks requiring a lot of thinking.

    It's going to take HOW LONG?
7. Loses things.

    How many times have I had to cancel and re-order credit cards?
8. Is easily distracted.

    I answered three "really important" (not) phone calls while typing this list.
9. Is forgetful in daily activities.

    Forget to eat lunch?

THE DSM-5 CRITERIA FOR A DIAGNOSIS OF ADHD:

Hyperactive-impulsive presentation:

1. Fidgets with hands or feet or squirms in chair.
   > I use a wiggle chair so no one will notice.
2. Has difficulty remaining seated.
   > Print things often so I have an excuse to get up—or just use a standing desk
3. Runs about or climbs excessively in children; extreme restlessness in adults.
   > What—adults can't climb or run around too?
4. Difficulty engaging in activities quietly.
   > Does quiet talking count?
5. Acts as if driven by a motor; adults will often feel inside like they were driven by a motor.
   > Racing thoughts, racing cars, racing ahead, vroooommmmm!
6. Talks excessively.
   > Who, me? Guilty as charged.
7. Blurts out answers before questions have been completed.
   > You mean I have to WAIT my turn? But what I have to say is really important!
8. Difficulty waiting or taking turns.
   > I already said this. Guess I was jumping ahead!
9. Interrupts or intrudes upon others.
   > You mean I am not the center of the universe?

COMBINED INATTENTIVE AND HYPERACTIVE-IMPULSIVE PRESENTATION:

Has symptoms from both of the above presentations.

Symptoms reprinted with permission from the Diagnostic and Statistical Manual of Mental Disorders, Fifth Edition, copyright 2013, American Psychiatric Association.

That's ADHD?

ADHD can look different in adults than it does in kids. It is often more subtle because as we have matured we have figured out how to mask and manage some of our challenges. Sometimes these challenges subside, and sometimes they are just expressed in new and exciting ways that can wreak havoc in our personal and professional lives.

I don't think the technical by-the-book diagnostic symptoms do justice to explaining what ADHD looks like in adults. Maybe you can see yourself in this list of "Adult ADHD" symptoms:

A. Prone to strong emotional reactions that take others by surprise both in their intensity and how quickly they dissipate. What's the big deal? (This is one of the most challenging symptoms of ADHD for many adults.)

B. Difficulty sustaining motivation on long tasks. Consequently, they may often seem to be doing a million things at once, jumping from one task to another. (Will you even sustain attention to read to the bottom of this list? I double-dog dare you.)

C. Bad finishers have many half-finished projects at home and work. They get bored once they have the project figured out or it becomes routine. This is totally me! In fact, the only reason this book got finished is because I told people I was writing it and was sick of feeling guilty for not finishing it!

D. Poor task initiators. They often drag their feet when starting tasks that require a lot of attention, that are mundane, or that are otherwise unmotivating. On the other hand, I can start a million projects that initially sound fun! (Go back to C to see how these million things end up!)

E. Yep, we can't start or finish—just bring us in for the fun parts in the middle!

F. Trouble sitting and reading. If they do read books, they may read several simultaneously and probably not finish most of them. If I can't sit through a meal, I certainly don't have the attention span and patience to sit and read a book. Ever stand up and read?

G. Regretful spontaneous purchases, large or small. A general inability to stick to a budget or an inability to mentally track how individual purchases fit into the bigger picture. My strategy is to just get what looks good and return anything that doesn't match once I get it home. Okay, I don't always return it.

H. Thrill-seeking behavior. This may be most obvious in physical tasks, such as motorcycle riding, bungee jumping, or other risky activities which result in frequent accidents and greater than average number of emergency room visits. However, it may also take place in relationships, such as by creating dramatic situations or breaking up when the relationship becomes familiar and routine. I love the thrill of a new relationship!

I. Feelings of inner restlessness and agitation. People with ADHD will often report that they feel they have multiple "tracks" of thoughts running through their head at one time.

Other "Soft" Signs

- Difficulty prioritizing. Ever forget a really important appointment because you were having fun? Often, people with adult ADHD misprioritize, failing to meet big obligations, like a deadline at work, while spending countless hours on something insignificant. Wait, who says fun is insignificant?

- High caffeine intake, perhaps because it's the only thing that helps them to focus. Is your favorite drink coffee or a carbonated fluorescent green?

- Intense dislike of social situations and "small talk."

- Sense of underachievement. People with ADHD often have difficulty achieving their potential at work, despite great mental effort. They may compensate by putting in extra hours to get the expected amount of work done. Also, they may find that it's helpful to come in early or stay late because they are less distracted when the workplace is quieter. This leaves NO time for play!

- Great difficulty functioning and being organized at college or in self-employment without external imposed structure or deadlines. This is why so many people with ADHD try the military!

- Low self-esteem due to experiencing more rejection and failure than most peers experience. They may minimize their strengths, always feeling that they could have done better. New failures and mistakes bring back to mind a laundry list of past blunders.

- Extreme distractibility. Wandering attention makes it hard to stay on track.
- Poor listening skills. Hard time remembering conversations and following directions.
- "Zoning out" without realizing it, even in the middle of a conversation.
- Hyperfocus—a tendency to become absorbed in tasks that are stimulating and rewarding.
- Tendency to procrastinate.
- Addictive tendencies—to substances (drugs, food) as well as activities.
- Frequently forgetting appointments, commitments, and deadlines.
- Constantly losing or misplacing things (keys, wallet, phone, documents, bills).
- Underestimating the time it will take you to complete tasks.
- Chronic lateness.
- Difficulty dealing with frustration or changes in plans.
- Hypersensitivity to criticism.
- Reckless driving and traffic accidents. ADHD makes it hard to keep your attention on a task, so spending time behind the wheel of a car can be hard. ADHD symptoms can make some people more likely to speed, have traffic accidents, or text and drive. Three speeding tickets in four months. Does that count? Going fast is the only way to stay awake sometimes!
- Tendency to seem "normal" when engaged in playful activities that hold their attention, make them feel motivated to continue, and are interesting!

In addition to the symptoms that are caused directly by ADHD itself, it may be of interest to you to note that it is uncommon for anyone—but particularly adults—to have symptoms of only ADHD. Most people with ADHD will have at least one other diagnosis. The challenges of ADHD alone can contribute to what are termed "co-occurring" or "co-morbid" diagnoses of depression, anxiety, and learning disorders. It is not unusual for adults to seek treatment for one of these problems only to find out later that the root cause is ADHD.

Symptoms Can Make You Special

The last few pages were about all of the "symptoms" and problems that ADHD can cause. If you think about when these symptoms show up most in your life you might notice a pattern—go ahead, think about it now. When do you struggle with focus and attention most? When do you have problems with motivation and sustaining effort? When do you tend to be more moody? When you are engaged in difficult, non-preferred, mundane, or boring tasks, symptoms such as distractibility, procrastination, inattention, or hyperactivity are likely to be most apparent.

Now think of a time when you totally rocked, a time when you were a superstar! You were on time, in the groove, and at the top of your game. I am betting that you were doing something you are good at, that you enjoy, with people you like (or alone), you were in a good mood, and maybe you were even having FUN! Did you struggle with distractibility? Did you feel unmotivated? Were you disinterested? Probably not. How did you feel? How did you handle problems? Playfully?

When you are in the groove, your brain is getting washed with dopamine and those symptoms that you struggle with during less-preferred tasks can be your greatest asset. For instance, what presents as impulsivity in one instance can give you the ability to be spontaneous, creative, and able to take a risk in a crisis.

Do you tend to be uber-distractible when you are disinterested and bored? Some might see your interest in many things, great imagination, and ability to see the potential and possibilities as inspiring.

Do you feel physically and mentally restless and have difficulty sitting still in long meetings? This same symptom can make you more energetic and enthusiastic, willing to embrace change, and capable of making intuitive leaps in a single bound!

Do you ever feel unable to take action on tackling a problem? Are you ever what some people call "stuck"? Are you accused of procrastination? That's because you have high standards, are excellent at getting things done on a tight deadline, and are capable of focusing intensely on a topic that has your attention.

It's all in the lens through which you view ADHD. And a great deal of the "management" of ADHD is in designing a life that keeps you interested and engaged and your dopamine flowing.

When you look at this, I hope the picture is starting to come in to focus for you. People with ADHD are at their best when they are engaged in activities that activate their brains and cause the dopamine to flow. The symptoms that can cause their biggest challenges can be transformed into their greatest assets. They are imaginative, inspiring, enthusiastic, playful superheroes! And they have a healthy aversion to all things mundane and BORING!

Doesn't that sound more like an advanced state of being rather than a disorder?

In fact, my friend Morgan suggested that we remove the DISORDER and rename this difference as ADHF—that is, Attention Devoted to Having Fun!

A lot of people have fun taking quizzes like the kind found in fashion magazines. So, just for kicks, we'll start with a True/False quiz.

Do You Have ADHD?

Answer these questions True or False **:

1. I would love to be a passenger on the space shuttle.
2. I like making my own decisions.
3. I have many "tracks" running through my mind at one time.
4. My vacations have to be planned.
5. I would choose hang-gliding over roller-blading.
6. I am a very creative person.
7. Adventure is in my genes.
8. I would rather be an accountant than a police officer.
9. I am known for being impulsive.
10. I do get bored easily.
11. I prefer to save money rather than spend money.
12. If asked to play board games, I would choose Monopoly.
13. I always look before I leap.
14. Extremes are part of my lifestyle.
15. I am comfortable speaking in front of large crowds.
16. I keep my opinions to myself; someone could be offended.
17. If going for a swim, I normally jump right in.
18. I prefer to get a weekly paycheck rather than work for commission.
19. I will never try skydiving.
20. I have a taste for ethnic and exotic foods.
21. I never drive more than 5 miles over the speed limit.
22. I sometimes text while I am driving.
23. My teachers often said I was not meeting my potential.
24. I tend to do well on tasks I am interested in and can barely stay awake for other tasks.
25. I have excellent anger management skills.
26. It often takes me much longer to complete tasks than I thought it would.
27. I would rather gouge my eyeballs out than clean my house.
28. It is important to follow rules.
29. I have felt that I am not meeting my potential.
30. When it is time to work, I can easily focus.
31. My attention can be quickly and easily distracted away from tasks.
32. I always do what I say I am going to do.
33. I can pay attention to long speeches.
34. When something is interesting to me it can be impossible to put it down until I am finished.
35. I am really smart, but I often forget things I thought I could remember.

36. I always know exactly where I leave my personal belongings.
37. I am often late to appointments.
38. I would rather put back my favorite ice cream than wait in a long checkout line.
39. If there is a problem in my relationship, it is usually my fault.
40. All of my projects are finished.
41. If someone gives me directions, I only remember part of them.
42. I prefer to get things done now rather than waiting until later.
43. I will clean my house instead of working on my taxes.
44. I have a hard time relaxing on vacation.
45. I have yet to find the PERFECT calendar system.
46. I am usually the one who has the most original idea.
47. I often see things that others have missed.
48. I wish I were MacGyver and could make anything out of a piece of string and a stick of gum.
49. I tend to pick up on other people's feelings easily.
50. When I am focused on a task, I hate to be distracted.
51. I prefer to work on one task to completion before starting anything else.
52. If I think I am right I will argue about even the littlest thing.
53. I focus best if I have music or another noise in the background.
54. I sometimes get off track while I am talking.
55. I am great at keeping track of time.
56. I have several organization systems but have never stuck with one for long.
57. The only way my bills get paid on time is if they are on auto-payment.
58. I buy presents for people in advance and then forget all about them.
59. I sometimes dial a phone number and then forget who I called before they pick up.

Answer Key:

1. T	11. F	21. F	31. T	41. T	51. F
2. F	12. F	22. T	32. F	42. T	52. T
3. T	13. F	23. T	33. F	43. T	53. T
4. F	14. T	24. T	34. T	44. T	54. T
5. T	15. F	25. F	35. T	45. T	55. F
6. T	16. F	26. T	36. F	46. T	56. T
7. T	17. T	27. T	37. T	47. T	57. T
8. F	18. F	28. F	38. T	48. T	58. T
9. T	19. F	29. T	39. T	49. T	59. T
10. T	20. T	30. F	40. F	50. T	

**This is not a scientifically validated test.

Scoring:
- One point for every response that matches the answer key.
- Add 10 points if it took you more than one sitting to complete the test.
- Add 20 points if you answered more than half of the questions randomly, without reading them, because you got bored.
- Add 30 points if you refused to take the test because you refuse to follow rules or directions!

Totals

0–20

You are likely "neurotypical"—any teacher's dream student.

21–35

You likely have some mild challenges with attention and enjoy getting a thrill now and then. While you are leaning in the direction of having diagnosable attention challenges, you are unlikely to meet the criteria for diagnosable ADHD. No meds for you!

36–60

Welcome to the tribe! You are more likely than not to have attention problems that are in the range of being "diagnosable." Hyperfocus when you are "interested" in something is common as are challenges with memory, interest, motivation, and focus when things are boring, routine, or just not your cup of tea.

61+

Holy cow! I should have listed this range first as people in this range are unlikely to make it to the bottom of the page to even read this!

CHAPTER 2
PLAY VS. WORK AND ADHD

Play is something that both animals and humans do naturally. We are wired to play. Not just because it's fun but because it helps us develop healthy bodies and brains, good social skills, resilience, and adaptability, and it prevents us from feeling depressed, lonely, and bored. That's why play is important for everyone. But it is especially important for people with ADHD, because play activates the dopamine system in our brain, naturally minimizes our symptoms, and makes everything not only fun but also easier. Yes, that's what I said: Play makes our brain work better, makes life fun, and it makes "work" easier.

By definition, play is "purposeless, all-consuming, and fun." Research with both humans and animals also demonstrates that play is a biological drive as crucial to our health as sleep or nutrition. Google "animal play"—the videos and images of animals at play will be enough to start activating your own dopamine, believe me!

Play is critical to healthy physical, mental, social, and psychological development. In fact, kids and animals who do not play tend to grow into anxious and socially maladjusted adults. Monkeys raised without any playmates tend to have many more social and physical problems than their playful peers, as noted in the "Monkeys Without Play" chapter of Play: Its Role in Development and Evolution (1976). Just the thought of those poor monkeys being raised without playmates is enough to shut down the dopamine in my brain! Likewise, in a study of twenty-six murderers Dr. Stuart Brown, of Stanford University, found that they all had two things in common: They came from abusive families and they did not play as children. The next time you feel guilty about wanting to play, realize that you are responding to your biological programming and that there is much to be gained by allowing yourself to play. Plus, no one wants to turn into a serial killer!

Although formal research on play as a distinct field of study is only in its infancy, many of the most recognized names in the field of psychology—including Freud, Piaget, Erikson, James, and

Vygotsky—included the importance of play in their theories of human development. What do they say? In a nutshell: Play is critical to human development.

Research in the field has established that play:
- Builds ability to solve problems, negotiate rules, and resolve conflicts
- Develops confident, flexible minds that are open to new possibilities
- Develops creativity, resilience, independence, and leadership
- Strengthens relationships and empathy
- Reduces stress
- Helps grow strong, healthy bodies

Research has also shown that children who play do better in school and become more successful adults. Through play, children learn to:
- Question, predict, hypothesize, evaluate, and analyze
- Form and substantiate opinions
- Persist through adversity

For both children and adults, play is at the root of creative thinking. Playfulness can help us do our jobs better and find more innovative solutions to problems. Play can help us be more adaptive, collaborative, spontaneous, and joyful. Research indicates that play can also be the antidote to isolation, worry, loneliness, fear, and violence. My own experimentation has shown strong evidence that play is the cure for lack of motivation, inattention, disinterest, and boredom!

I get asked by a lot of adults: "What do you mean by play?"

Play is… fun!

Simple as that.

What do you think of when someone says "Let's play?" Acting silly? Being irresponsible? Being non-productive? Kicking a ball, running around, playing tag, trying to avoid cooties? I know if asked to "play," most of my adult friends immediately think of sex! But, for me, play is anything that makes me feel alive, awake, clear, happy, engaged, energized, focused, and motivated. (Yes, that includes sex.)

Play can take many different forms, including humor, adventure, physical, competition, creativity, storytelling, collecting, and performing. It can be social, creative, digital, active, and intellectual. It can happen at home, at work, outside, inside, with other people, or by yourself. While propriety may require that you "take things seriously" in some settings, there is no end to the possibilities for how, where, and when to play.

How do you know if you are engaged in play or being playful? Is being tickled until you are ready to pee in your pants play? Can you be playful while working on an accounting spreadsheet? You have to know what we are talking about so you can have some gauge and goal to know when you are acting in a playful way. Play workers—remember play is not the opposite of work, so this makes sense—have debated and written extensively about their ideas of what play is. Here are the most consistent characteristics of play according to "the experts." Ironically, the "experts" are all adults!

Play is:
- Apparently purposeless (done for its own sake); there is no "end goal."
- Voluntary—no one has to force you, entice you, or blackmail you to get you to play.
- Inherent attraction—it just looks fun!
- Losing track of time—during play we can become so absorbed in what we are doing that we lose track of time (this sounds like hyperfocus, right?).
- Diminished self-consciousness—who cares if you trip, fall and land in a puddle of mud, as long as you get up and keep going?
- Improvisational potential—we aren't locked into a rigid way of doing things; we are open to "winging it" or to chance.
- Continuation desire—you'll want to play more.

So, back to the questions I asked above: Can you be playful while creating an accounting spreadsheet? Could you imagine creating a setting and process for this task that would make it meet the criteria of play? It can be done!

As humans we are capable of choosing how we approach any task. Can you remember dreading a task that you normally might have enjoyed because you were afraid of being judged or didn't like your co-participants? On the flip side, perhaps you have gone to an event that you expected to find tortuous and you ended up having the time of your life because you ran into a favorite person or were taken by surprise by the event itself. Any task or event can be approached as an opportunity to play.

The bottom line is that play is about mindset. It is not only what you do but how and what you pay attention to. It's taking an ordinary conversation and seeing the fun in it. Sometimes the play is solitary, and other times it is social. Sometimes it is for all the world to see, and other times it is internal. I will be talking more about a "playful mindset" later in this book, so hold on, buckle yourself in, and keep moving forward!

In The Playful Path, Bernie DeKoven writes:

SPREADSHEETS CAN BE FUN! YES!

Be-fore you even get started you may want to Google "Excel fun" or "Excel games" to realize that Excel is not just for spreadsheets anymore. Once you are done having fun and the dopamine in your brain is flowing, you probably want to get back to creating your spreadsheet. Have fun with this too. You can use a variety of colors, make comments into various shapes and colors (hearts, stars, thought bubbles), color each cell or column a bright color, or give headers unique names that make you smile (don't worry, you can replace these later). Besides the spreadsheet itself, you can also make the setting you are in more conducive to fun. Create a spreadsheet playlist of music that will keep you focused and energized. Throw in something that will make you take an occasional break to get up and dance! Doing boring tasks with another person also affords many ways to make the task more fun.

"It's not like one of those paths you read about, like a spiritual path, or anything to get religious about. It's more like a way to be on whatever path you happen to be on at the time: a, you know, playful way. You're walking down a street. It's the same street you've walked down before. It's not like you have to find a different street. But this time, you walk a little more playfully. You step on cracks. You walk around a tree, twice. You wave at a bird."

The Playful Path includes many examples of ways to play. I frequently apply one such method when I have to drive in city traffic. Traffic is my least favorite thing about being in a city. There are days when I am stressed and will sit and comment out loud at the horrible drivers, idiotic pedestrians, traffic lights, and the world in general and how it is getting in my way. But on a good day I will remember to play a little game: I make up stories, the more ridiculous the better, about the people around me and their situations. Perhaps one of them is missing an eye (poor thing) and can't actually tell that I was on his left side as he cut me off when he tried to merge into my lane. He lost his eye in a terrible accident involving a tiger; it's all just too horrible to describe here. But I couldn't help but take pity on him as he drove right in front of me.

Keep It to Yourself

Everyone can play, whether you are an introvert or extrovert, the class clown or a wall flower. You don't have to be the life of the party to have fun. At a social event, sometimes I like to stand against the wall and listen to what others are saying and giggle to myself rather than really getting involved in the conversation. I still consider this to be play and fun in the moment. Play is not always about moving around, being loud, or even interacting with another person. Not everyone is suited to this style of play and not every situation is appropriate for active play.

Humans have a seventh sense- imagination. It allows us to form pictures of the future in our mind. It also allows us to change details of memories from the past to create new stories. We can use our imagination to play with what is in front of us or imagine what would amuse us in another time. Mentally manipulating what is in front of you can be very playful. Imagining someone as a particular animal, deconstructing things into parts and reassembling them differently in our mind, or "seeing" music in colors and patterns. These are all internal ways to play.

There are many reasons for playing in a quieter way or independently. Some people are shy. Sometimes we just don't feel like playing with others (even I have days when I don't want to talk to anyone!). And sometimes we find ourselves in situations where playing "out loud" may not be acceptable—if you're somewhere quiet like a library or serious like a wake.

But even when we don't want to play with others or play actively, we still benefit from using play to engage our brains, relieve boredom, problem solve, and just have fun. I often think of funny things and can be found sniggering to myself. It's sometimes irritating to have someone ask what I am thinking—because it's not as funny out loud or because I would have to explain all the thoughts that led to the moment of humor for it to make sense. So just laugh to yourself if you catch me chuckling; don't stare or point your finger, because then I will just get paranoid (you know what I'm talking about).

Why We Stop Playing

As adults we believe we have to be taken seriously to be successful. But research shows that, like kids, adults benefit enormously from playing—in all aspects of their lives and in all relationships. A playful person is more attractive, productive, creative, and fun!

When did play move to the bottom of your priority list? Probably about the time that being happy became second to being productive.

Ironically, it may interest you to learn that play may be the cure to low productivity, unhappy relationships, boredom, and depression. Research shows that when you're stressed, the brain's activated emotional hub, the amygdala, suppresses positive mood, fueling a self-perpetuating cycle of negativity. Yuck! Play can break you out of that straitjacket.

Play is crucial to the well-being of adults. So why do we stop playing? Kids say, "Let's play!" When was the last time you said that to anyone?

As children, it was our job to play—tag, hide-and-seek, monkey-in-the-middle, imaginary scenarios to slay the neighborhood dragon, and other fun activities. But we all have to "grow up." As we progress in school and later move to our chosen occupation, our focus typically shifts toward being successful and being evaluated as competent. We take tests, have interviews, and apply for acceptance into various organizations. We are told that we can play when our "work" is done, whether we're talking about schoolwork, homework, or housework. "Work first, then play," we're told, unless the play is educational or productive. The underlying message is that play for the sake of fun is a waste of time, because every moment spent playing is a lost opportunity to get ahead in life. We learn to fear failure and to be wary of looking "silly" in front of our peers. The more task-oriented we become, the less we engage in play activities. When adult responsibilities consume us, we stop playing. (Do you remember being a kid and wanting to be a grown-up? Did you think this was what you were in for?)

On average, Americans have thirteen paid vacation days per year, and most people don't even take all of them. Other countries have forty days. We take our weekends to play hard, but that's really to let off steam from our play-deprived lives and just get enough energy to get back into the ring. If you work for yourself (which I do), weekends are often not sacred, and play almost always gets pushed aside in favor of productivity. Once this happens, you are doomed—doomed I say, doomed!—to a life of drudgery, depression, failure, stress, health problems, and failed relationships. (Are you feeling motivated to play more yet?)

Finally there are the ambiguities that seem particularly problematic in Western Society, such as why play is seen largely as what children do but not what adults do; why children play but adults only recreate; why play is said to be important for children's growth but is merely a diversion for adults.

—*Brian Sutton-Smith,*
  The Ambiguity of Play

The "Dandy Horse"

Adults often want to avoid the appearance of being too playful for fear of being labeled as "immature" or "slackers" by less playful adults. But the truth is that playing is enormously important to our well-being as adults. Through play, we manage stress, solve problems, learn, and foster physical health and healthy relationships. Just as in childhood, play as an adult can lead to greater creativity and happiness.

Being playful at work is not only good for your health, it is also great for morale, productivity, and creativity. Play has become a powerful word in leadership circles. It has been touted (pause for a moment and just think about that word—"touted"—weird, right?) in popular media sources as "the number-one leadership competency of the future," "the key to a company's success," and "the greatest natural resource in a creative economy."

The design company IDEO is a world leader in creative innovation of products. Their founder David Kelly and CEO Tim Brown have given some pretty spectacular TED talks about creativity and play. Not surprisingly, IDEO has implemented some guidelines for their brainstorming sessions that start with having "playful rules." Their suggestions include:

- Go for quantity
- Encourage wild ideas
- Defer judgment
- One conversation at a time

They encourage interactions by having people build off of other people's ideas. They also use both visual and physical mediums to illustrate the ideas. Facilitators draw diagrams, storyboards, and role play.

It may be obvious why we don't play at work. But many adults don't play when they have leisure time either. They sit in front of the TV; do "research" on the Internet; exercise; or sit around eating and napping. While sometimes your brain may need a rest, sometimes it needs some dopamine. And, believe me, other than some forms of exercise, none of those activities is going to make your body produce more dopamine.

Play Is Sometimes Just Fun!

I live near a local park and in the summertime there are far more adult sports happening on the fields than there are kids' sports. The adults have ultimate Frisbee, kickball, softball, hula hooping, and group runs. I have friends who year-round enjoy line dancing, concerts, art walks, ballroom dancing, traveling, and many more "playful" activities. Often these are about getting together with friends and being social. Other activities are about leaving behind stresses of daily life or just stresses of the day. They are done for the sake of enjoyment, relaxation, changing mindset, and just feeling good. There is nothing better than smiling, laughing, and forgetting everything else to enjoy some playtime.

Of course there is one playful activity that is reserved strictly for adults (or should be), and that is sex. If sex is not playful, you are definitely doing it wrong. Go back and look at the definition of play. This is ideally the state that you want to be in for a healthy and enjoyable sex life. According to Dr. Ari Tuckman, "Sex is the playground of adults!" (more about this later).

So remind me what your argument is to explain why you aren't playing more…

Perhaps now you are starting to see the benefits of asking a friend, "Want to play?"

Proof That Play Can Make You an ADHD Superstar

There is a plethora—funny word! It sounds like it should have a texture—of research supporting the idea that from play we learn the rules for social interactions, cooperation, planning, negotiation, self-management, frustration tolerance, conflict resolution, and problem solving. We also develop our executive skills through play. Yep, I snuck that one in there. If you know ADHD, you should know about executive skills. The skills—sustained attention, emotional control, planning, persistence, mental flexibility, social thinking, and

metacognition (being aware of your own thinking)—are at the root of many struggles faced by kids and adults with ADHD. It's true. Play, especially free play, helps us develop and engage our executive skills. When we are playing the challenges of ADHD are less likely to get in the way and we are best able to learn.

There are many sources that someone with ADHD can find to learn about how diet, exercise, food, and medication impacts symptoms. There is also a plethora written about the impact play has on early development and adult well-being, the neurochemical impact of play on the brain, and the neurobiology of ADHD. However, there is little written about the connection between ADHD and play. In reading all of this information one might conclude that connecting play to ADHD is a "no brainer."

When you are playing, your brain gets a rush of dopamine, the "feel good" neurotransmitter. This is the primary neurotransmitter linked to ADHD. Dopamine production that accompanies a playful mood leads to improved executive functioning, including increased attention, motivation, ability to persevere, and improved problem solving and resiliency. Studies show that playfulness can increase performance on the job and stoke creativity by breaking up the mental set that keeps us stuck. It resets the brain. Heaven knows there are many days when I wish I literally had a "reset" button on my brain. Who knew it was labeled "play"?!

Despite this obvious connection, there is little formal research directly connecting play and ADHD. I guess there isn't enough money in fun—which is free—when you compare it to the millions we spend on medication to treat ADHD.

But, stage left, here comes our hero! Dr. Jaak Panksepp has looked directly at play as a way to manage ADHD. He has done this through his research with rats—yes, we humans and rats have similarities in our brain structures!—which suggested that among rats who were artificially "given" ADHD, those who were allowed to play more were able to function better as adults than those who were prevented from playing.

Sergio Pellis, a researcher at the University of Lethbridge in Alberta, Canada, has found that play specifically develops the prefrontal cortex, the seat of the "executive control center" and the site that is impacted in ADHD. Specifically, he said that the socially reared rats with damage to prefrontal cortex act like normal rats deprived of play as juveniles. His findings have implications for the human world and suggest that children with greater opportunity to engage in free play, especially rough housing play, are socially more proficient and score better in their academic work. Engaging in play develops the prefrontal cortex and enhances the executive function of this part of the brain, enabling improved emotional control and impulse control, which leads to improved attention and decision-making.

That's all I have to say about that! These two guys—the only two scientists who have formally researched and made the connection for us between play and ADHD—are in agreement.

The concept that play helps us to overcome some of the executive skills deficits present in ADHD is supported by the research of Lev Semyonovich Vygotsky(1896–1934). He observed that in play a person is able to resist impulses by using fantasy and self-imposed rules. For instance, you may be playing a game with a friend. If you keep winning every time, eventually your friend won't want to play. So if you play less aggressively, you can keep the game going because both of you are now having fun. This is an example of a self-imposed rule. The urge is to win every time, but instead you stop and think about what it will take to continue the fun. This is also an example of practicing an executive skill of impulse management. By doing so the players are meeting their potential, rather than acting impulsively. Vygotsky suggested that we are able to show our best selves when we are engaged in play (Google "Zone of Proximal Development"—I never thought I would tell someone that!).

There it is: Research, evidence, proof that play can be used to treat your symptoms of ADHD! When you play, you are at your best. You are better able to plan, organize, make decisions, focus, pay attention, remember information, juggle multiple tasks, and adapt. And, last but not least, you're more fun to be around! This is when those symptoms of ADHD can become what makes you sparkle.

I've done my job, so why aren't you playing right now? Oh, right— you're still operating on old messages. We need to talk about those.

Programmed to Play… But Rewired to "Work Hard"

As kids we are all programmed to play. It is a natural state of being and interacting with the world. It is how we develop and learn about ourselves, other people, and the world. We are born curious. We learn early in our lives to ask questions such as "why?" "how come?" and "when will we be there?" We make believe, use our imaginations, build things, pretend, and create pictures for our parents to hang proudly on the refrigerator.

Then we go to school to learn. (Here, the music in my head changes to one of impending doom.) Sure, maybe the first year our learning is couched in some forms of play. We have lots of recess, art, music, and story time. Despite all this fun, we learn. We learn to follow rules, get along with friends, listen, focus, pay attention, and much more. Then we have to learn not only to listen to stories but to know our letters and learn to read and write. Sometimes there is some fun built into this, but often this is when we start to learn about "hard work." The kind of work where you have to sit still at a desk for periods of time, listen to the teacher, and do what we are told. No talking to your friends. No goofing off. Oh, yeah, there will be a test on this and your parents will be told about whether you are keeping up with the rest of the class or not (sometimes called tattling). The "normal" kids may not enjoy this as much as play, but they adapt. At this age you may not know if you are in the ADHD tribe yet, but your teacher might notice that you seem to drift off, can't sit still, and maybe even get irritable when it's time to "work."

The traditional educational experience is focused on cramming information into our heads, making us spit it back out, and making sure we "behave" while we do this. As you progress through the grades, the environment for learning becomes increasingly mundane. Learning is often rote. Teachers have to make sure we meet standards. So we are taught what is on the test. Some classes are a bit more fun. (Chemistry! Let's experiment! Gym! Let's play! Art! Wait, does your school still have this?)

Sir Ken Robinson gave several brilliant TED Talks criticizing our current approach to education (another Google alert!). He argues that our education system is antiquated and designed to address the learning style of the "thinkers" and to ignore the learning abilities of the more creative members of our population. In a talk called "How to Escape Education's Death Valley," Robinson says, "If you sit kids down hour after hour and give them low-grade clerical work, don't be surprised if they start to fidget!"

What happens when a kid starts to fidget or can't focus any longer? Their name gets written on the board, they have to stay in from recess, and they are told they need to work harder and stop goofing off. They are kept from play and punished by being subjected to more of the very environment that caused their problem with focus and fidgeting rather than helping them figure out how to learn differently. As children we are taught to think that our naturally playful state of being is something to be ashamed of. We are told that we have to do things like everyone else or there is something wrong with us.

When I was in elementary school I was fortunate to have teachers who were big on experiential learning. In fact, in third and fourth grade I was in an open classroom. My teacher, Mr. Bergraff, was a caring, patient man who loved teaching. The room was set up with a rope swing, bean bag chairs, a piano, and bunnies (a couple at first and many more by the end of the second year -- those were some playful bunnies!). I learned to play chopsticks on the piano. I did a presentation on cumulus clouds. I learned from visitors who came to talk to us on a regular basis. I also learned how to work in a team, how to problem solve in new ways, how to keep an open mind to differences in other people, and the importance of moving around to help myself focus. Learning was fun!

Unlike Mr. Bergraff's classroom, our education system generally takes a "one size fits all" approach to learning. Robinson suggests that we need to personalize learning. Imagine that! Taking into account how each of us learns and where our interests and abilities lie. Who says learning by sitting at a desk and focusing for long periods of time is the "right way" to learn? What if cave men acted like that? They would have been extinguished by predators and none of us would be here today.

Q: If we lived in a primitive hunter/gatherer society, which kids would grow up to be the best hunters, the best trackers, the best builders, the best fighters, and the best storytellers?

A: The same kids who are labeled with a learning disorder today.

So what happens to many of these kids who are shamed into trying to be traditional learners and taught that their naturally playful state is something to suppress? They struggle in school. They feel inadequate, stupid, and bored. Some of them become the class clown to mask their discomfort. Some become bullies so no one will tease them for being slow or stupid. Some of them zone out. And some of them turn to other sources to try to feel better. Research studies find that 25–35% of people with ADHD abuse substances. People with ADHD also have a higher rate than their non-ADHD peers of engaging in risky behavior, overeating, and having other addictive and unhealthy behaviors. While we may see these as self-destructive, if you ever take a moment to ask someone why they do these things, most will say "to feel better."

Trying to fit in and feeling out of sync with most people around you is not a pleasant experience. It's like being the only one who dressed up for an event in the most outrageous Halloween costume you could find, only to learn as you entered the room that you were attending a formal dress function (and all you have on underneath is your superhero underwear!).

If this traditional environment is not conducive to activating our ADHD brains and making us feel good, why then as adults do so many of us choose work settings that perpetuate this same problem? We work at 9-to-5 jobs, with short lunch breaks, having to sit at our desks, attend meetings, fill out reports, follow protocol, do things the way everyone else does, and—heaven forbid—maybe even work in a gray cubicle! We don't take breaks and don't make time for fun because we have to work longer hours to keep up with our co-workers. We choose to work hard.

For adults who ignore their need for play and do not take into account how their brain functions best, the consequences can be apparent in failed relationships, difficulty sustaining employment, depression, anxiety, financial problems, substance abuse, and other addictions.

What if you choose to do things in a way that turns your brain on, rather than trying to just do what seems to work for everyone else? What if you could stand at your desk and dance while you worked instead of sitting on your butt all day? What if rather than being serious and "working hard" you could be more productive by returning to your naturally playful state of being? Do you remember what it felt like to be playful? To enjoy learning? To feel like your brain was turned on, your thinking was clear and focused, and you felt motivated and happy to be productive?

Beating the Work-Harder Troll into Submission

The case has been made for play. It's fun, it activates your brain to help you overcome the challenges of ADHD, and it can make you more productive, creative, and improve your mood. Then why don't we all "just do it"? I'm betting that even if there is a playful angel sitting on one of your shoulders saying "let's play," there is a really old, wizened troll sitting on your other shoulder repeating all those messages that you heard as you have grown up. (Imagine this is said in the gruffest, growly troll voice: "You can do better, don't goof off, get busy, grow up already, this is serious.")

If you look back in your life at times when you were successful, you may see, like I have, that play, in one form or another, has been the key to many of those wins. Let's play "Whack a Troll!" -- like Whack a Mole, but you're beating that nasty serious little troll into submission!

People with ADHD struggle to demonstrate their intelligence. Often we don't do well on tests or other pressure situations. How many times have you heard, "Your child is so smart, she's just not meeting her potential. If only she would work harder." This was most likely a teacher in a subject you did not prefer. Or a boss on a task that was boring. Really, they want us to "work" harder? One of my mentors, Jeff Copper, has said, "If you're working hard, you are focusing on the wrong thing."

I have long told people that I was generally an A student in high school. However, reality was not the same as my memory or perception of myself. Not long ago my father sent me my report cards from middle and high school. Shocker! I was a B student, with A's in classes that were challenging, interesting, or taught by an inspiring teacher. I earned an A when I had to take third year French—having never taken a foreign language before—because it was a challenge to keep up with my peers. Being challenged is playful to me. After this year of learning French, I had little interest in the subject and generally earned only passing grades. Essentially, when I was having fun, I was learning and able to demonstrate what I had learned. Far from being disappointed that I was not such a great student, I was thrilled that my grades showed what the research about ADHD has shown time and again. Turn my brain on, and I'm brilliant!

Since high school I have worked in many jobs and taken on many tasks. I went to college and graduate school (my eight-year-long challenge thanks to a high school teacher who told me not to go into psychology). I started my own practice, then stopped offering therapy because it was no longer interesting to me. Instead, I started a nonprofit working with adolescents involved in the corrections system. Now that was fun! This held my interest for a full five years. Most jobs lasted less than two years because they weren't interesting or fun anymore at that point. I also hate working under someone else's rules. For several years I have been working for myself and have been having a ball. What can I say? I'm an awesome boss!

Imagine that your "job" was to think about, notice, find, and do "play" all day. This is the job I created for myself. Do people say I am not smart? Nope (maybe behind my back?). Are my ideas taken less seriously? Not as long as I am willing to take the first step to implement them. Does anyone say I am not meeting my potential? Or that I should "work harder"? Certainly not. Most people think that I am one of the hardest working people they know. I think this is funny—because I do everything I can to avoid "work." Sometimes I tell people my little secret: I am really lazy. I hate working hard. Don't get me wrong; I do what some people consider to be "hard work." But in any "work" I do I want to be efficient and inspired, and I want to have fun! So, it's not really hard at all.

One of my earliest idols is Mary Poppins. She has an inspired quote, "In every job that must be done there is an element of fun. You find the fun, and—snap!—the job's a game!"

About 60% of adults with ADHD have either been fired or changed jobs as a result of ADHD symptoms, according to a 2011 study released by the ADHD Awareness Coalition ("Staggering New Statistics About ADHD," ADDitude, October 11, 2011).

Adults with ADHD have significantly more experiences of behavior problems, being fired or forced to quit, voluntarily quitting due to boredom, and being reprimanded in the workplace, according to the University of Massachusetts Study on Adult ADHD, conducted from 2000 to 2003 (ADHD in Adults: What the Science Says, page 7).

Time and again articles have been written about high-level CEOs and other adults with ADHD that point to the repeating pattern that when an adult with ADHD is focusing in their area of interest and allowed to work in the way they work best they are highly productive and have workplace longevity. A Forbes article even referred to ADHD as a "superpower" ("ADHD: The Entrepreneur's Superpower," May 14, 2015). When we are involved in tasks that that make us feel motivated, interested, and focused, "work" feels more playful and less like work ("ADHD in the Workplace," D Magazine, July/August 2011).

Think about a time when your boss (or, if you work for yourself, circumstances) demanded that you engage in a task that you really enjoyed or something that you are good at. What was your attitude toward the task? How did you approach it? Think about the properties of play—natural attraction to the task, wanting to continue, lack of feeling self-conscious, voluntary, focusing on the moment... Did these apply to how you engaged in the task?

Now think about a time being handed a task that you dread or just isn't your "thing." If you're like me, you focus on getting it over with, feel obligated to do the task, and hope you don't screw it up. I might procrastinate (nooooo!), take a lot of breaks and have difficulty starting back up, and my attention is going to be easily redirected to anything else. Heck, I have even been known to clean when I don't want to do another task. And I hate cleaning. This is not play. And my ADHD is at its worst in this situation. Play can make work more productive and pleasurable.

This is the paragraph you bring to your boss to convince her or him that they should incorporate more play in the work environment, hire more people with ADHD, and buy them all a copy of this book.

(Writing that was a moment of play for me. While sitting down for long periods of time to write can sometimes feel like a job, when I can spontaneously incorporate an idea that brings to mind an amusing image for me, it feels like play. And not just for the moment—it helps to carry me forward as I get back to the "serious" part of writing as well!)

A moment of play in the midst of "hard work" can improve your energy, creativity, attention and focus, and engagement in a task. Some might criticize that playing at work is akin to "slacking off," but more informed people will recognize it as an investment that pays off in more productivity. While a moment of play can have short-term dividends, research shows that when you take a vacation from work—even a four-day weekend—you are more inventive, productive, and healthier (fewer sick days) when you return. Some play is good, and more play is even better!

I hope that the playful angel on your shoulder has grown in strength and perhaps even cajoled the evil ugly troll with all the negative messages about play into playing a game of hide and seek. If so, don't go find him. Let the troll stay hidden. Start creating new messages for yourself about the value of play in your life. Perhaps maybe even put reminders of these new beliefs around you at home and work. And if that troll decides to come out of hiding, play Whack a Troll with him!

CHAPTER 3 - TURN TO PAGE 69

REMEMBERING HOW TO BE PLAYFULLLLLLLLLLLLLLL

TURN TO PAGE 70

Bored to... Idears?

Recent studies on boredom and creativity suggest that boredom can actually enhance creativity ("Does Being Bored Make Us More Creative?"; "Approaching Novel Thoughts: Understanding Why Elation and Boredom Promote Associative Thought More than Distress and Relaxation"). Investigators have found the boredom we experience during passive activities (like reading boring reports or listening to a long dull speech) motivates people to seek out new and rewarding activities. In other words, an unoccupied mind will seek a way to play.

"The more a person limits himself, the more resourceful he becomes. A solitary prisoner for life is extremely resourceful; to him a spider can be a source of great amusement. What a meticulous observer one becomes, detecting every little sound or movement."
—*Søren Kierkegaard, Either/Or (1843)*

It's somewhat ironic that I was sitting in the most boring conference (on ADHD) while writing this chapter. My brain was on fire! It was only after I wrote most of this section that I realized that I was experiencing exactly what I was writing about!

So while boredom can be the spark for some people developing bad habits, when we use this down-time to get creative and play, we can find that we get some of our best ideas and engage in the most fun and mischievous play because our brains want to be engaged.

Think about it—what do you do when you are bored? Most of us tolerate this state for only a brief period of time and then start to look for ways to "do something." Boredom is a great motivator! This is when it is a great habit to have a "Plan to Play" with a list of ideas at hand. You guessed it. There is a section in this book that will guide you through creating your very own plan. If you just can't wait to get started, jump ahead!

up of many components. By practicing some of these characteristics, you become more playful and it may feel more natural to take on your bigger play goals. For instance, you may want to engage in more playful social activities, such as playing on a local adult kickball league. If you are not ready to put yourself in front of the pitcher or out in the field, maybe you want to attend the games of your favorite team, volunteer to be the ball person, or bring the team snacks.

Here are some of the qualities and habits of playful people that you may want to start incorporating as part of your current habit loop.

Characteristics of Playful People:

Focus on the process not the goal

Focus on the effort not the outcome

Optimistic attitude

Reframe things in a positive manner

Combine things in unexpected ways

Use positive language

See failure as an opportunity to-

-improve

Enjoy learning

Celebrate wins and failures with-

others (Google "failure bow")

Embrace change

Practice playing

Sensitive to others

Observe others playing

Build breaks and down-time into-

their daily routine

Curiosity

Persistence (remember the phrase

continuation desire?)

Laugh at themselves

Seek novelty

Ask questions

Explore

Play games

Enjoy competition

Are spontaneous

Take risks

Don't fear being criticized

Smile

Are kind to others

Aren't judgmental

Adapt and make do with

what is at hand

Jan was finding it increasingly difficult to feel focused, motivated, and interested in projects she once enjoyed. Everything seemed to take extra time and energy.

Jan came to coaching because she was no longer enjoying the work she was once passionate about. When she started coaching we spent some time identifying some of the work and play habits she wanted to incorporate or eliminate and her specific markers for success. Once this was established, we created a habit loop for Jan to adopt healthier work habits. Jan's first cue was her alarm, which was set to times of the day when she wanted to make sure to take breaks. When her alarm would go off Jan would take a break for five minutes and engage in a playful task from a list she had created. Her reward was resetting, rejuvenating, and relaxing her body and mind so that she could be more productive, not feel tired, and avoid evening fatigue. She found that another reward was that she was getting back in touch with friends who she enjoyed spending time with, having more quality time with her partner, and reconnecting with her co-workers who often had valuable input into her projects.

Jan did find that she sometimes was in the middle of a task and would ignore her alarm. Once she created back-up reminders that went off two minutes after the first alarm, she was making her goal of taking breaks every two hours almost all the time. Jan also found that by changing the sound of the alarm at the beginning of each week she was less likely to ignore it. Jan found that the breaks made her so much more productive and inspired that she expanded them to ten minutes and then fifteen minutes over time. Jan eventually came to see these breaks as a necessary part of her work day and she no longer needed an alarm to remind her; they had become a valuable habit.

Like Jan, you may find it hard to just dive into the play pool. Diving in is one way to develop the habit. But you might want to just wade in at the shallow end. Here's what I mean: People who tend to be more playful have certain characteristics. And being playful is made

You might put this on a bright piece of paper, write it in bold colors, put it in various places you know you will see it during the day. Because we tend to become blind to things when they remain the same for periods of time, make sure you change it up when the reminder becomes less powerful for you. Move the visual reminder someplace new or use a different alarm sound, for instance.

In addition to using the habit loop to adopt a playful attitude, there are other factors that are crucial to adopting a habit.

The first is "You must believe!" Hallelujah! [Come on, imagine music is playing, hands are clapping, and the chorus is singing your praises.] You must BELIEVE that you can change, that you can be more playful. Having belief in yourself can be powerfully influenced by being part of a group. Interacting with other people who are playful or are focusing on becoming more playful can increase your experiences of playfulness and therefore your belief that you are capable of being more playful. It's also true that when we commit to others our intention to adopt a habit, we are more likely to follow through than when we keep our plans to ourselves. So announce it out loud: "I will be more playful starting now!"
Your neighbor probably thinks you're crazy now, but, hey, you're going to be more playful.

All Work and No Play... Makes Jan a Dull Girl

I was working with Jan, an ambitious salesperson who was successful in most areas of her life. She had a great relationship, was top in sales at her company and was generally healthy. The one thing holding her back from feeling at her best was her work habits. Jan would often go the entire day forgetting to take breaks because she was "on a roll" at work. At the end of the day she would be exhausted and would feel unmotivated to do anything other than get a quick bite to eat while watching TV and then get herself to bed. The next day she would get up and do this all over again. All work and no play was making Jan a dull and unhappy girl and a very boring friend and partner. At work, time of day? Where will you be? Who will or won't be present? What do you want to accomplish? What feeling state will trigger the habit?

REWARD: What reward will you get or give yourself for engaging in this habit? Habits that result in an intrinsic reward are often most powerful (intrinsic is a big word for saying "natural"—for instance, the "intrinsic" consequence of not wearing your coat in January if you live in Maine is that you will be cold). Play, by definition, should involve natural motivation and desire to continue for its own sake—not because you will get candy (chocolate?!) for doing it but because it's enjoyable.

ROUTINE: In the case of play, routine is strongly tied to the reward you want to experience. The type of play routine you engage in will depend on whether you are wanting social interaction, mental stimulation, laughter, physical stimulation, relaxation, or some other reward.

So how can you remind yourself to practice being playful? Sticky notes! Alarms! Reminders from a friend! Or an easy positive reminder such as:

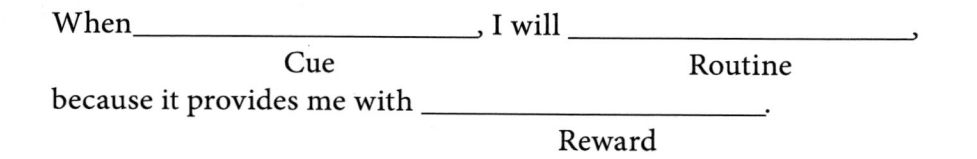

When_____, I will _____,
                Cue   Routine
because it provides me with _____.
                                     Reward

For example: When I feel bored, I will walk around the block once, noticing all the things that are purple around me, because it provides me with a feeling of energy and wonder.

Or—
When I can't motivate myself to clean the bathroom, I will put on my bathroom cleaning playlist, because it provides me with the stimulation and energy and fun I need to do the job.

play more and then—bing bang boom!—we would just do it. But the reality is that we make a plan to get up and exercise every day and maybe we get up three times that week and get our sneakers on to make breakfast and never even make it to the gym.

While it would be great to live in an ideal world where habits were easy to break and create, the reality is this is going to take some intention and effort on your part, even if ultimately it's fun! I want to give you permission to start by being spontaneous in your efforts to be more playful. You may already have some ideas that keep popping into your head about how you want to be playful. Go ahead and set an intention to be playful next time you have a free moment. You might feel spontaneously inspired to be playful once you start, or it might be a while before you think to use your time this way again. This is a way to dip your toe in the water of being more playful. Like any change, the more you practice the quicker the habit will develop and become second nature for you. If you want to put in the effort to make being playful your new habit I have some suggestions.

I read a few books and a lot of articles about developing habits as I was doing my research for this book. Some of them had "8 Steps to develop the habit of..." And others had "10 Steps to develop...." Those all sounded like a lot of work, so I opted for "Three steps to develop a habit!" This is based on Charles Duhigg's The Power of Habit: Why We Do What We Do in Life and Business.

1. Identify the Cue.
2. Identify the Reward.
3. Identify the Routine.

Okay, there is more to it than that. But these are the three elements you need to focus on. These three elements are parts of the habit loop.

CUE: To adopt a habit we first need to identify a CUE. To do this we need to consider one or more of the following triggers for the habit: Time, place, people, desired outcome, and mood or feeling. So what have Super Dooper Pooper Scooper Party each weekend (dog poop patrol). This works best in the warm months when we can put on some music as we have a "treasure hunt" for dog poop. Even the dogs get in on the fun! Sometimes I even put on my favorite rain boots and a funny hat to get me in the party mood!

Getting in the Habit Loop

Being playful is a skill and, like any skill, you can get better at it with practice. The more you practice the more you develop certain pathways in your brain and the more automatic this type of mindset and behavior becomes. At first it may take effort, more for some people than for others. Over time it becomes easier. The more you do it, the more being playful becomes a habit.

The good news is that, unless you are a serial killer (if you missed this reference go back to the beginning of chapter two), you likely played as a kid. As a result of this play, you developed strong neural connections, or pathways. Those pathways are still there! Research has found that the way we played as kids is often related to the ways we like to play as adults. These pathways have just become a bit overgrown with gobbeldy-gook (a scientific term for boring, adult stuff). With a bit of activity on the path, the way will become clear again. You will rediscover these pathways in an exercise later in this book.

I am going to go out on a limb here and assume that when you really think about creating a new habit, you think, "This is going to be work." I don't want to minimize the effort that creating a new habit takes. Doing something new is a change, and change takes effort. In an ideal world we could write a plan to lose weight, manage time, or

1. First, you have to recognize your current mindset about taxes that is making this such a drag.
2. Then decide if you want to do your taxes the same old way this year (this is a yes-or-no question).
3. Assuming you decide that you want to shake things up, next ask yourself when have you had fun working on a large project? Where were you, who were you with, what was going on around you, what made it fun or interesting?

Once you have a good list of ideas, make a plan to get your taxes done with fun!

Face it, taxes are boring. What is the opposite of everything you have come to associate with doing your taxes? Being with friends, having fun, feeling energized, wanting to fill out the long form just so you can continue the good times—have a tax party! Every year around tax time we have a big tax party. Everyone brings their tax documents, computer, snacks, calculator (or smartphone), and limited alcoholic beverages. Some people like to have music playing and others want a quiet space. But we are all doing our taxes, holding one another softly accountable, and taking breaks to have fun. You don't have to have a lot of people to have a party. Sometimes it's just me and one friend. Other times it's twenty people or more all doing our taxes at the same time. What's on your taxes? What is the most outrageous deduction you're taking this year? All fodder for tax party fun!

This is just one idea to make what can otherwise be a painful, uninteresting, demotivating task more fun. Read on to get more ideas about how to approach work and everyday life in a more playful way!

Last year I met a fantastic teacher, Sarah Kesty (sarahkesty.com). You can see two 1-minute interviews with her on the PlayDHD Youtube channel. In one of them she talks about how when she is working with kids she can make any task seem fun by making it into a party. For instance, a clean-the-classroom party! Put on some music, make a conga line, and get kids to pick up items and put them away as they pass by. In my home we

There is no "right" or "wrong" answer. No one is all serious or all playful And you may shift along the serious-playful continuum depending on the situation, your mood, your focus, who you're with, or how you slept that night. The most important thing is to recognize where your current mindset is so you can decide to change it if it is not serving you. Just as they say about a map, "You can't get where you want to go if you don't know where you are."

"Play is training for the unexpected."

—Marc Bekoff, evolutionary biologist

Would You in a Box, in Your Sox, with a Fox?

In my coaching with adults with ADHD I often have clients who are unhappy at work, in their relationships, and in general. When I ask them how they play, many of them are at a loss. In fact, many of them say they don't play at all! At least this is how they feel. When we get down to it, we always find ways that they play, even if they are not obvious or frequent.

And then there are those tasks that are challenging for even the most playful to find fun. Tax season is a big challenge for many of my clients. There is nothing less fun for most people with ADHD. Doing taxes requires us to pay attention to details, gather receipts and records from the piles, organize them into categories, and work on filling in documents with numbers for long periods of time. Argh! Most people think that there is a correct process for doing taxes that involves sitting alone in a quiet room for hours at a time sifting through the piles of papers and persevering until you have all the boxes filled in. But what if taxes were fun? You don't think that's possible? I argue that if you have a playful mindset, anything, even taxes, can be fun.

SCORING KEY:

Go to question number 12.

If you answered "Yes" you are a highly playful person.

If you answered "A Little" you aspire to be playful and may be more prone to watching others rather than joining in.

If you answered "Nope" you need to go back to the start of this book and start over again. Just kidding.

How did you approach the quiz? Did you answer according to the way you are now or in the more playful way you want to be? Did you realize that you do a lot of things that are associated with being playful already? Or that there are simple things that you can do to be more playful? Maybe you decided to tell someone a joke or just try to "lighten up" a bit today! Part of taking the quiz is to help you gauge where you are. But quizzes also sometimes give you ideas about areas to focus on to become more of how you want to be—in this case, more playful.

How do you use this information to develop a more playful mindset? Change the messages in your head!

Do you tell yourself "I'm smart" when you succeed and "I'm an idiot" when you fail? Or do you give yourself credit for the effort you made in either case?

Do you give yourself a pat on the back for taking on a challenge even if it doesn't end in the result you were hoping for? Or do you beat yourself up for taking on more than you are capable of?

When you fall short of your goal are you still excited that you learned something new, or is the goal the only marker of success?

Do you approach a task looking forward to who you are working with, what you might learn, and the fun of the process? Or do you focus on just getting to the end goal?

A. I don't do that too much.

B. Of course!

- Do you still feel childlike joy?

  A. Yes, constantly.

  B. Sometimes.

  C. No, not really.

- Do you tell jokes?

  A. Yes, daily.

  B. Every so often.

  C. Not really.

- Do you have fun with your friends?

  A. Always.

  B. Most of the time.

  C. No, not really.

- Do you enjoy playing games of some sort (board games, video games, sports)?

  A. Yes, definitely.

  B. If I'm in the right mood.

  C. No, not really.

- Do you find it easy to let go and have fun?

  A. Absolutely.

  B. More or less.

  C. No, not at all.

- Do you feel like you have enough time for play in your life?

  A. Yes.

  B. Sometimes.

  C. No.

- Do you have fun outdoors?

  A. Yes.

  B. Once in a while.

  C. Not especially.

- As you were taking this quiz, did you have fun thinking about times when you played and enjoyed yourself?

  A. Yes.

  B. A little.

  C. Nope.

about exercise? I can tell you that when I start a new exercise routine I usually dread it. My mindset is, "Exercise is hard work." But once I have a routine and start feeling stronger and have more endurance I look forward to exercising. My mindset shifts dramatically! Of course, sometimes our mindset is the result of a conscious decision to be or think a certain way because we want to make changes in our life or to who we are. The obvious one is work vs. play. I definitely grew up learning the mindset that "working hard" was more valued than "being playful"—and that these two were mutually exclusive. I decided to let go of this mindset and adopt a more playful persona in order to have a happier—and, ironically—more productive life.

In her book Mindset, Dr. Carol Dweck talks about people having either a fixed mindset or a growth mindset.

I think of them as the serious and playful mindsets.

A serious mindset puts enormous pressure on the person and can lead to anxiety and depression because the outcome of any task is thought of as being a reflection of the person's worth and ability. Yuck! You may think, "It's not really that bad." If so, stop reading this book and come back when you decide you want to have more fun.

Quiz: Which One Are You?

MINDSET QUIZ
- How do you feel now
  A. Curious.
  B. Impatient.
- How often do you smile when you are alone?
  A. Quite often.
  B. I don't know if I do that.
- Do you laugh easily?
  A. I am not sure.
  B. Yes. I crack up all the time.
- Do you enjoy telling funny stories?

It's All in Your Mind(set)

What's the difference between having a serious and a playful mindset? People do not necessarily have one or the other, but knowing the difference can help you to adopt a more playful approach to life. (What is your "mindset" about learning this concept right now?)

Your mindset is a way of thinking that determines your outlook, mental attitude and behavior. It is your set of personal rules, philosophies, expectations, and beliefs about yourself, other people, and the world around you. We all have mindsets that affect our expectations, interpretations, and actions in our parenting (spanking or spoiling), at work (follow the rules or be a rebel), at the grocery store (organic or as many preservatives as possible), in the bathroom (toilet paper over or under), and all other aspects of our life. Many adults have a mindset about play that they apply to themselves and others. This mindset often revolves around the misperception that "play is for kids." Can you imagine what that mindset would lead to? Oh. I guess if you are reading this book you actually might be living by this mindset. My mindset about that belief is, "That sucks!"

So where did your mindset come from? Was it pre-programmed into your brain before you were born? Is it because your mother dressed you in hand-me down clothing? Or perhaps you learned it from your crazy Aunt Mirna? Likely, all of this and more has had an influence on your current mindset about various aspects of your life. For instance, money—whether you are frugal or free with spending your money, you were likely influenced by your parents' attitudes about money. Statements such as "Money doesn't grow on trees," or "You can't take it with you," influence whether you are a saver or a spender. These kinds of experiences help shape your money mindset.

Sometimes we adopt mindsets after being exposed to a one-time powerful experience or from repeat exposures to more subtle influences over time. You might develop a mindset about not liking to go to the circus if one time you were scared by a clown. But what

How can you define playfulness for yourself?

Think of someone you know who you consider to be playful. What qualities or characteristics does this person exhibit? _____

_____

_____

What is it that makes you enjoy their company? _____

_____

_____

How do they play? _____

_____

_____

How can you use this insight to guide your own play? _____

_____

_____

When will you do this? _____

_____

_____

Who will you play with? _____

_____

_____

How will you play? _____

_____

_____

_____

_____

Now, remember to make a plan, write it down and share your commitment to play with others.

CHAPTER 3
REMEMBERING HOW TO BE PLAYFUL

You have the evidence that play is to ADHD the way insulin is to a diabetic. You have been asked to consider the horrible, dreadful possibilities of a life of struggle, boredom, and underachievement if you continue choosing to do things in a manner that does not take into consideration your brain's need for more stimulation. But this is not just about playing. In fact, it's more about being playful—having an approach and mindset about making any task or activity more interesting and fun. So many definitions. While the list could go on, what I realize is that ultimately, when people try to define "play" or "playful", it really comes down to a feeling we get when we know we are engaged in such activity or have adopted such a mindset.

---

play·ful [pley-fuh l]
adjective
: fond of games and amusement; lighthearted.
: intended for one's own or others' amusement rather than seriously.
: giving or expressing pleasure and amusement.
: happy and full of energy; eager to play
: showing that you are having fun and not being serious
: full of play or fun; sportive; frolicsome
: experimental
(Sources: Google, Dictionary.com, Merriam-Webster, Thesaurus.com)

Playfulness is the quality of perceiving everything that happens in a way that is playful. Playful is an attitude, not an action. You can approach anything with a playful attitude, even "work." Heck, if you were really gutsy, you could even approach a court date with a playful attitude. When you adopt a playful attitude you don't have to rely on external props, such as a set of jacks, a hula hoop, an app on your phone or even another person to be engaged in play. And playfulness does not have to be expressed outwardly; sometimes it's how you think about things.

CHAPTER 4

THE WAY BACK PLAY MACHINE

The key to being playful is that you have to know what game you are good at—that is, what type of play you enjoy. If you try to play in a way that you don't enjoy, you won't be able to get to that state of playfulness, flow, or fun that makes play... well, play! Remember, play is purposeless, voluntary, and attractive. During play you lose awareness of time passing, you are free from fear of failure, you adapt to changes, and you are motivated to continue playing. These are the defining characteristics of play.

Imagine that you have horrible stage fright. Your boss asks you to do a role play in front of your peers. Likely, you are not going to find this a pleasant or fun experience. You might stutter, give one-word responses to his prompts, and want this over with as quickly as possible. This is NOT PLAY! If, on the other hand, being a performer is something you find exciting you might ham it up and enjoy the opportunity to ad lib in front of your peers.

Mihaly Csikszentmihalyi—try saying that even one time fast!—is known for his theory of "flow." Flow is a state in which "a person performing an activity is fully immersed in a feeling of energized focus, full involvement, and enjoyment in the process of the activity." Sounds like play, right? Relative to games and play, he writes that in order to enjoy the optimal level of play and learning, the activity must have an appropriate level of challenge for the player's skill level. Too much of a challenge and the player becomes anxious; too little challenge and the player becomes bored. When you hit that sweet spot, the player can truly play.

When considering how to approach a task playfully, it is important to know where your skills and interests as a player lie so that you have the best opportunity to experience the task as play—that is, to get to that state of flow. Likely if you have been out of practice playing for a while you may not know what types of play you can choose from, much less what type of player you are. Well, step right up, buckle yourself in and hold on for a wild ride... we are going to go back, back in time...

Picture this: You are in a doctor's office and the receptionist hands you a stack of paperwork to fill out. Included in this is your health history. How many times have you been in the hospital? Did anyone in your family suffer from lazy eye? How many times have you been pregnant (this is a trick question for men to see if they're paying attention, right?). Filling out a "health history" is a dreary business. Essentially, what you are being asked is, "What do you think your risk is of being a sick patient?" Not this ride... this is boring!

Now imagine being in a different doctor's office—maybe my office. But this time you are handed a single piece of paper and asked to take a walk down memory lane and to write down the times in your life when you had fun, times when you were successful, enjoyed yourself, felt wild abandon, and were most playful. Start at your earliest memories and work your way forward.

Our history is a link to who we have become. There are moments in our lives that contribute to who we are today. Taking a "play history" is an opportunity to connect with the playful and fun memories of our past so that we can remember what makes us feel most alive. We can then use this to guide our plan for how we play as adults.

Taking a Play History

You're going to put this book down and take 15 to 20 minutes to play with this. But—whoops!—first you need to read the rest of this page.

Identify times in your life when you remember having fun. Think about what you did as a child that really got you excited, that really gave you joy. Write those down.

Start with the earliest memories you have of playing as a kid. Note every significant detail, even the things that seem silly or irrelevant but come to mind anyway. Try to come up with three to five memories of playing. If you feel stuck, use these questions:

- Who was there?
- Where were you?
- What were you doing?
- How did you feel?
- How did you start?
- What "props" were you using?
- What was the best part?

Just put down everything you can think of without trying to decode the meaning.

Now, can you see the common theme among these activities? For instance, if one of your themes from playing as a child is being a performer in the company of others, you might enjoy taking acting classes, joining a flash mob event, or organizing your friends to participate in a local talent contest.

If, on the other hand, you have always tended to prefer playing by yourself and you are more of an explorer you might enjoy building cities with Legos (the community of adult Lego fanatics is huge!), traveling to new places on your own, or investigating problems.

When I went through this exercise years ago, a few memories emerged:

I thought of how much I loved dressing up with all the vintage gowns in my grandmother's dress up chest as a kid.
I thought of how much I loved acting on stage.
I thought of how I now love to dress up and have become known for the fantastic hats and fascinators I wear to conferences and events (and sometimes in my day-to-day life).
One of my prominent themes is Performer.

Here is my friend Jeff's Play History, as he wrote it:

As I think back, here are a few of my favorite play moments:
Playing with friends with toy construction equipment on a dirt pile in the back yard. We also liked playing with Hot Wheels and Matchbox cars (I had a huge collection). We would play with them daily, always taking turns picking our cars for the day. Everyone always wanted to pick the cop car to enforce the rules of our game.

My friends had a huge collection of Legos, we used to build planes and spaceships out of them.

I loved playing soccer so much so that I built my own soccer goals in our backyard when I was 12. I asked my mom to buy the materials (PVC pipe, netting, etc.). The very first shot by my friend hit the underside of the crossbar and it popped off... and then with a creaking noise, the whole goal keeled over and collapsed to one side. Back to the drawing board. This time, I had Mom get me cement and some nuts and bolts. With the goals planted into the ground, our summer days of backyard soccer began.

My friends and I also built a tree fort in the woods. All by ourselves (crooked cuts in the wood and all). We spent many days playing war and hanging out in our fort.

When I was younger, my sister and I would put on "shows" for our siblings. Sing and dance (mostly jumping on the bed) with our LightBrite as our spotlight.

Self-assessment (play types): I would say looking across all of my activities (beyond just the ones listed above), I'm a "mutt" of sorts: Director, Explorer, Competitor, Collector (Hot Wheels), Performer.*
*(Jeff has read ahead and is referencing the Play Personalities that you are about to learn in the next section!)

GYPSY

FORTUNE

TELLER

Who
are
you?

Play Personalities

If you read the previous chapter—and I don't assume, because that makes an ass…. You know the rest—you have a fresh memory of some of your early and most enjoyable play experiences. You may have many giddy memories of discovering abandoned caves, creating works of art, entertaining the masses, and other forms of play. How do you categorize these and know what type of play is going to be the funnest (yes, I meant to say that) for you? Many people know exactly what type of player they are. But for others it's good to have a template of sorts to get started. Knowing what type of playfulness you are drawn to can give you a direction to start out on your quest to be more playful.

Welcome to the world of "Play Types" (as opposed to types of play). This is basically your "Play Personality." Based on neuroscience and natural behaviors observed in both animals and humans. The Play Personalities listed below are based on Dr. Stuart Brown's original eight from his book, Play, How it Shapes the Brain, Opens the Imagination, and Invigorates the Soul. But Eight Is Not Enough! So I have added one more: The Performer (just because this is my book and I can do whatever I want!).

As you read through these you may notice that many of the play personalities have overlapping qualities. For instance, you can be engaged in both Kinesthetic play and Competitive play when you play a sport. The Storyteller and Artist/Creator play personalities both use their imagination to create and engage in their respective forms of playfulness. It would be odd—and rather rigid of you—to find that your brand of playfulness only fits into one of these nine play personalities. Take your time and reflect on how you engage in each of these types of play. Pay attention to how these memories feel. Are they exciting? Joyful? Motivating? Enticing? Do you find yourself imagining future plans that fit into one of these play types?

The Joker

The most primitive and extreme player throughout history is the Joker. The Joker has one goal: to be entertained. They are often restless, feeling bored with the simple humdrum of everyday life where others might be satisfied. They're quick-witted inventors with tongues as sharp as their intellect. Outgoing, friendly, and accepting, the joker's play involves drama, practical jokes, and other active modes of nonsense. They find humor in all aspects of life and love to make other people laugh. April Fool's Day is the Joker's favorite holiday.

If you're a Joker, you might want to:
- Join an improv troupe.
- Go to a comedy club.
- Tell a colleague a joke.
- Wear a clown nose to your next board meeting.
- Make up alternative lyrics to a favorite song.

The Explorer

Explorers like to focus on what could be rather than what is. They see many possibilities in everything they can sense, experience, and imagine. Explorers are enthusiastically and outwardly focused on the future and like to initiate change. They see every situation as an opportunity to try something different. Curiosity leads to playful exploration of the world around them. The Explorer loves an adventure. Exploration can take place in either the physical or the intellectual world.

If you're an Explorer, you might want to:
- Try a new restaurant or travel down a road you have never gone down before.
- Rent a bike in a new city and get a little lost.
- Travel locally, nationally, or internationally and meet other travelers through TravBuddy (www.travbuddy.com) and Couch Surfing (www.couchsurfing.com).
- Run a science experiment.
- Attend a Startup Weekend event to explore entrepreneurship (startupweekend.org).

The Kinesthete
Kinesthetes are people who like to move. They learn by "doing"—through active and physical interactions with the world around them. Kinesthetes enjoy pushing their bodies to their limits and feeling the results. The Kinesthete is at play and in their glory when engaged in physical activities such as sports and other exhilarating experiences.

If you're a Kinesthete, you might want to:
- Take dance lessons.
- Join an outdoor activity meetup group.
- Go running.
- Have a party at a local rock gym or trampoline park.
- Buy a trampoline for your yard.

The Competitor

The Competitor enjoys competitive games and plays to win. Being number one, the strongest, most powerful, fastest, or richest are all motivating. Playing on their own or as part of a team, the Competitor loves to take on a challenge. The Competitor's games extend beyond athletic playing fields to video games, poker, and the stock market.

If you're a Competitor, you might want to:

- Host a night of board/video games.
- Join a team sport.
- Watch a sporting event with friends.
- Time yourself on any task, and try to beat your own best time or race against someone else.

The Artist/Creator

The Artist finds their playful joy in making something out of nothing! They can take ordinary objects and put them together to create magical works of art. Creative Play extends beyond art to a world of music, dance, composition, construction, electronic gadgets, gardening, knitting and decorating are also in their purview. The Artist admires beauty and creates it in many forms.

If you're an Artist/Creator, you might want to:

- Build, make, and hack your own creations—sand castles, cakes, or animated creatures!
- Join a community garden and grow your own salad makings.
- Find a local art studio and take classes.
- Build something spectacular with Legos.
- Design and create a website.

The Director

The Director is at play when they are in charge of planning and executing events—whether it's a weekend away with friends or a large corporate initiative. Directors are dreamers but goal-oriented and have a desire for a prominent role in a group or organization. They live in a world of possibilities where they see all sorts of challenges to be surmounted, and they want to be the ones responsible for surmounting them. They are "take charge" people.

If you're a Director, you might want to:
- Start a meetup group.
- Plan and organize an event.
- Direct a project.
- Oversee the remodeling of a house (yours?).
- Apply to become the Director of Chaos at New Holland Brewing Co. in Holland—yes, this is a real job title at this company!

The Storyteller

For the Storyteller the imagination is the key to the kingdom of play. Storytellers are, of course, authors, playwrights, and cartoonists as well as journalists and photographers. But they are also those whose greatest love is reading those books or watching the movies—people who make themselves part of the story and who experience the thoughts and emotions of the people in the stories. The Storyteller loves to create imaginary stories for the pleasure of others. The Storyteller is also an individual who make up stories in their minds to explain things they're experiencing or to entertain themselves.

If you're a Storyteller you might want to:
- Join a writers' group or book club.
- Go to a local poetry reading.
- Take a creative writing class at a local university.
- Put together a photo journal of an event or trip so you can share the story with others.
- Submit a local interest story to your local newspaper.

The Collector

The Collector
The thrill of play for the Collector is to have and to show off the most interesting collection of experiences or objects. The key is that both the act of collecting and the thing they collect puts them in a play state. The Collector enjoys collecting things for fun and sometimes for profit. Coins, toy trains, old hats, wine, shoes, ties, classic cars, limited edition anything—it's all exciting for the Collector.

If you're a Collector, you might want to:
- Check out a flea market or map out a yard sale itinerary.
- Go to a classic car show or event with other like-minded enthusiasts.
- Surf eBay looking for the best "stuff" to add to your collection.
- Visit the Spy Museum in Washington, DC, to see a large collection of cool vintage spy gear.
- Start your own collection of navel lint (Google Graham Barker's Navel Fluff Collection). Or some other strange collectible.

The Performer

The Performer is someone who loves people and new experiences. Performers are lively and fun and enjoy being the center of attention. They live in the here-and-now and relish excitement and drama in their lives. The Performer enjoys being spontaneous and sees the whole world as a stage. This is the type of person who likes to put on a show for others—think of actors, models, musicians, and public speakers.

If you're a Performer, you might want to:
- Give a TedX talk.
- Put on a play with your kids.
- Make a YouTube video for the world to see.
- Perform at open mic night at a local comedy club.
- Learn to perform magic to amaze your friends and family!

Although your play preferences may change somewhat with age, it is likely that they are rooted in what you liked to do as a child.

Most of us probably are a combination of two or more play types.

What types of activities have always brought you pleasure? As you were reading this, was there a play type that made you start remembering being particularly playful in the past? Or one that made you smile as you imagined engaging in some playful fun in the near future? This may be a clue to the type of player you are at heart.

Bulls Eye!

Anyone who knows me will tell you that I like to compete. Turn anything into a challenge, and I'm all in. It turns on a switch in my brain (dopamine?). One of my favorite people, John, enjoys shooting guns. He offered to take me to the outdoor shooting range and let me "try" some of his guns. Ooh, loud noises and shooting things! Fun! This was a new experience for me, and, unfortunately, my aim sucked.

But then John asked if I wanted to have a "friendly" competition—the winner would buy ice cream. He would even let me have a closer target if I wanted—NO WAY! Round one, I hit 7 of 10 shots on the target area. Being a good sport, John offered to increase the fun by making it best two out of three magazines. The second round was a tie at 8 apiece. Now, he will deny this, but I beat him! First time shooting and I hit a bullseye! (In my imagination, it was the eye of a bad guy.) That was the best ice cream ever! I do give John credit for being a great instructor.

ADHD Players Throughout History

Imagine a world population that includes 8 percent of people with ADHD, who are capitalizing on their unique strengths because they have the inside scoop about play. Not only would people with ADHD rule the world, the world would be a much more playful place to live. All kidding aside, you may not "rule the world," but you could be the next Sir Richard Branson, Steve Jobs, Michael Jordan, Jim Carrey, Jamie Oliver, Will Smith, Michael Phelps, Ty Pennington, Terry Bradshaw, or James Carville... Artists, athletes, geeks, politicians, actors, builders, all at the top of their profession and all of them have ADHD. Not so ironically, I would think of each of these people as having a fun personality.

"The same genes that are involved in ADHD can also be associated with risk-taking behavior. While these urges can be problematic or even self-destructive—occasionally leading people into delinquency, addiction, or crime—they can also lead to earth-shattering breakthroughs in the fields of art, science and exploration."

—Professor Michael Fitgerald, MD

As you've look through this book, you may have noticed the names and descriptions of people on some pages. Was this a random act of distraction on my part? Nope! All of these people are either diagnosed or hypothesized to have characteristics of ADHD, and they have contributed to the world as we know it in big ways. That is to say, you are in good company! You are part of a strong and vital tribe! People with ADHD are creators, inventors, explorers, and visionaries. We propelled progress by taking risks, thinking outside the box, and daring to dream big. If you are looking for a role model with ADHD, you won't have to look far. Many of the inventions, amazing feats, and mind-blowing concepts from these famous people past and present are the result of their love of play in all its various forms. They reflect the gamut of play personalities you just read about.

On the following pages is a list of people who are either diagnosed or hypothesized, based on historical reports, to have characteristics of ADHD. These people have all contributed to the world as we know it in big ways. That is to say, you are in good company! You are part of a strong and vital tribe! People with ADHD are creators, inventors, explorers, and visionaries. We propelled progress by taking risks, thinking outside the box, and daring to dream big. If you are looking for a role model with ADHD, you won't have to look far. Many of the inventions, amazing feats, and mind-blowing concepts from these famous people past and present are the result of their love of play in all its various forms. They reflect the gamut of play personalities you just read about.

NEANDERTHAL MAN

Neanderthal Man... Creative, interested in new things, funny, not keen on rigid tribal organization or rules, empathetic, energetic both mentally and physically, bored very easily.[1]

One of the hallmarks of ADHD is impulsivity. Picture this scenario: Herd of mammoths seen grazing. Cavemen prepare to hunt. Mammoth herd stampedes. Cavemen impulsively leap into action and cull mammoth. Those who leapt into action most quickly and starred in the cull were clan heroes. The caveman equivalent of sports heroes. ADHD, therefore, was probably historically a genetically advantageous feature.[2]

Neanderthals were thrill-seekers -- adrenaline junkies. (Much like some of our ADHD heroes of today.) They loved battle, and music, and had a tendency to incite chaos. New DNA data reveals that many of us are carrying Neanderthal genes. And not only that, but evidence is mounting that when those genes are activated in you, they can cause you to become incredibly resourceful, pioneering, creative... and unpredictable.[3]

NOMADS

Nomads - A genetic variant associated with ADHD has been found at higher frequency in more nomadic populations and those with more of a history of migration. Evolutionary anthropologist Ben Campbell of the University of Wisconsin—Milwaukee, studied the Ariaal, an isolated nomadic group in Kenya. His findings suggest that hyperactivity and impulsivity—key traits of ADHD—have distinct advantages to nomadic peoples. Increased impulsivity, novelty-seeking, diffuse attention, ability to adapt to changing environments, aggression, and high activity levels may help nomads obtain food resources, adapt to new environments, and exhibit a degree of behavioral unpredictability that is protective against interpersonal violence or robberies. From studies of modern hunter-gatherers, we can surmise that learning took place through play, observation, and informal instruction, rather than through the highly regimented classrooms.[4]

1451-1506 - CHRISTOPHER COLUMBUS

Christopher Columbus, perilous adventurer,

In 1492 Columbus sailed the ocean blue.

(we didn't even have to google that one!)

1452-1519 - LEONARDO DAVINCI

Leonardo Davinci- Italian painter, sculptor, architect, musician, scientist, mathematician, engineer, inventor, anatomist, geologist, cartographer, and botanist;Mona Lisa,(1517) Last Supper (paintings). Invented Ornithopter 1871

Ben Franklin- Founding Father USA, Political Theorist, Inventor - Bifocals (1770), Franklin Stove, and Lending Library (1731)

1756-1791 - WOLFGANG MOZART

BEN FRANKLIN - 1706-1790

Wolfgang Amadeus Mozart Started playing the harpsichord at the age of three. He was composing his own piano pieces at five, symphonies at nine and whole operas by the age of 12. Wolfgang never went to school, but was home-schooled by his dad. His best known pieces are The Marriage of Figaro (1786) and Requiem (Mass for the Dead) Mozart is described as having immature behavior and creative intensity. He could get lost in his work and often made jokes that were silly and unexpected. His impulsivity and mood swings also suggest he may have been in the ADHD tribe.

Lewis Carroll- English Author, Logician; Alice in Wonderland (book 1865), "Jabberwocky", "The Walrus and the Carpen- ter" (poems)

1832-1898 - LEWIS CARROLL

Thomas Edison, inventor 1,093 patents (singly or jointly) and was the driving force behind such innovations as the phonograph, the incandescent light bulb and one of the earliest motion picture cameras (kineto- scope 1893) ."To invent, you need a good imagina- tion and a pile of junk." "I never did a day's work in my life, it was all fun."

ALEXANDER GRAHAM BELL - 1847-1922

THOMAS EDISON - 1847-1931

Alexander Graham Bell - awarded the first U.S. patent for the telephone in 1876. As a child, young Bell dis- played a natural curiosity about his world, resulting in gathering botanical specimens as well as experiment- ing even at an early age. From his early years, Bell showed a sensitive nature and a talent for art, poetry, and music that was encouraged by his mother. With no formal training, he mastered the piano and became the family's pianist. Despite being normally quiet and introspective, he reveled in mimicry and "voice tricks" akin to ventriloquism that continually entertained family guests during their occasional visits.

Henry Ford, industrialist and founder of Ford Motor Company raised on a farm, he found farmwork not to his liking. Preferring instead to hunt and fish. Invented the Quadricycle (car) in 1896. August 1918- Edison and Ford are two of the "vagabonds who headed a convoy of 8 vehicles through 4 states as they stopped to camp on farms, examine old industrial sites, take hikes along rivers, and (as one series of photographs documents) partake in playful contests measuring skill with farming implements.

1863-1947 - HENRY FORD

Albert Einstein, physicist- Conceived of a little thing called the "theory of relativity" (1911) Einstein famously came up with some of his best scientific ideas during his violin breaks. "Play is the highest form of research."

WILBUR AND ORVILLE WRIGHT - 1867-1912

ALBERT EINSTEIN - 1879-1955

Wilbur and Orville Wright (1871-1948)- Inventor, Airplane (1903- first flight), Three Axis Controller.

Pablo Picasso- Founder of the art movement known as Cubism. Famous quote: "Every child is an artist. The problem is how to remain an artist once he grows up."

1902 - 1984- ANSEL ADAMS

PABLO PICASSO - 1881-1973

Most famous painting: Guernica (1937)

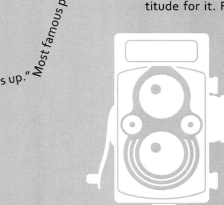

Ansel Adams - American photographer and environmentalist. His black-and-white landscape photographs of the American West, especially Yosemite National Park, have been widely reproduced on calendars, posters, and books. Adams was an energetic, inattentive student, and that trait coupled with a possible case of dyslexia earned him the heave-ho from private schools. However, he was obviously a sharp boy when motivated. When Adams was just 12 years old, he taught himself to play the piano and read music, and quickly showed a great aptitude for it. For nearly a dozen years, Adams focused on little other than his piano training. Photography was something he did for fun. It was never intended to be his profession but demand for prints of his Yosemite landscapes soon produced all the income he needed and he eventually embraced photography as his sole occupation.

Salvador Dali - A visionary artist, uninterested in conven-
tional norms, he pushed the
boundaries of art and be-
came the most famous
surrealist of them all.
Most famous for the
painting Persistence
of memory 1931.

1904-1989 - SALVADOR DALI

MALCOMB FORBES - 1919-1990

EVIL KNIEVEL - 1938-2007

Evil Knievel - On September 8, 1974, with much media fanfare, dare-
devil Evel Knievel tried and failed to leap the mile-wide chasm of the
Snake River Canyon on his specially engineered rocket motorcycle
(skycycle). He suffered more than 433 bone fractures in his career,
thereby earning an entry in the Guinness Book of World Records as
the survivor of "most bones broken in a lifetime"

Malcomb Forbes- Publisher of Forbes magazine (1957-1990). known for extravagant
spending on art, travel, and parties. Quote:
The biggest mistake people make in life is
not trying to make a living at doing what
they most enjoy.)

1000
0101
1101
0101
1011

1946- CRAIG VENTER

Craig Venter-biologist and genomic research pioneer- Venter himself recognized his own ADHD behavior in his adolescence, and later found ADHD-linked genes in his own DNA. As a genomics expert, Venter mapped the human genome, created "synthetic life" and put his signature int this be creating a "watermark" written into the DNA of a cell containing the code table for the entire alphabet with punctuations, names of 46 contributing scientists, three quotes, and the web address for the cell... How creative! [5]

PAUL ORFALEA - 1947

Paul Orfalea, founder of the copying empire, Kinko's. The idea for Kinko's came to Orfalea in 1970, while he was a student at the University of California at Santa Barbara. He noticed all the people lined up to pay 10 cents a page to use the library photocopier. He decided he could provide the service cheaper. Orfalea borrowed $5,000 and opened his first Kinko's in a converted hamburger stand near the university. It was equipped with a lone Xerox machine. Today, his copying empire, which FedEX now owns, is worth $2.4 billion, and Orfalea, 56, has retired. [6]

Richard Branson - from starting his own space exploration company to owning his own island. Virgin Records, Virgin Airlines, Virgin Mobile. You never know what he's going to do next... Virgin Space Resorts (this isn't even far fetched!).

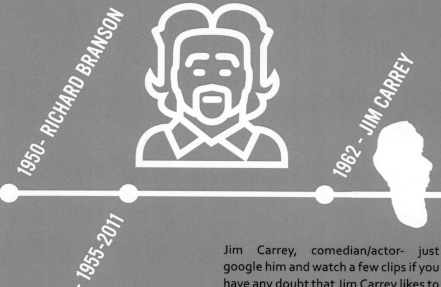

1950- RICHARD BRANSON

1962 - JIM CARREY

STEVE JOBS - 1955-2011

Jim Carrey, comedian/actor- just google him and watch a few clips if you have any doubt that Jim Carrey likes to play. He remembers coping by being the class clown, and said that it's "hard for me to come down from what I do." That hasn't stopped him from putting out some of the most epic comedies of all time and acting like a complete nutcase wherever he goes. ADHD works well for him. The Mask (1994)

Steve Jobs- an American pioneer of the personal computer revolution of the 1970s. He had difficulty making friends with children his own age, however, and was seen by his classmates as a "loner". As Jobs had difficulty functioning in a traditional classroom, he frequently misbehaved and was suspended a few times. His father (who was abused as a child) never reprimanded him, blaming the school instead for not challenging his brilliant son enough. He grew up on a farm in Wisconsin, bore a resemblance to James Dean, had tattoos, dropped out of high school and traveled around the midwest for several years looking for work. He went on a blind date with Clara Hagopian (1924–1986). They were engaged ten days later and married in 1946. (impulsive?).

OK... the fun has really gone out of this history of ADHD section for me (too long!) So we are going speed things up a bit and take a shortcut to the finish line.

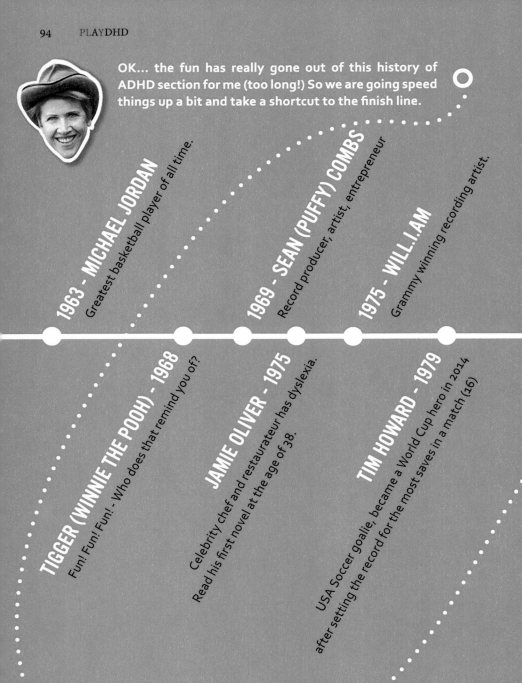

1963 - MICHAEL JORDAN
Greatest basketball player of all time.

1969 - SEAN (PUFFY) COMBS
Record producer, artist, entrepreneur

1975 - WILL.I.AM
Grammy winning recording artist.

TIGGER (WINNIE THE POOH) - 1968
Fun! Fun! Fun! - Who does that remind you of?

JAMIE OLIVER - 1975
Celebrity chef and restaurateur has dyslexia.
Read his first novel at the age of 38.

TIM HOWARD - 1979
USA Soccer goalie, became a World Cup hero in 2014 after setting the record for the most saves in a match (16)

1979 - ADAM LEVINE

Lead singer of Maroon 5 and a vocal coach on the popular TV show The Voice

1985 - MICHAEL PHELPS

The first American to win eight medals in a single Olympic Games in Athens in 2008

PERCY JACKSON - 2010

Percy Jackson and The Olympians 1st Super Hero with ADD/ADHD and Dyslexia.

SHANE VICTORINO - 1980

Golden Glove Outfielder MLB. Boston Red Sox World Series title.

BART SIMPSON - 1987

Bartholomew JoJo "Bart" Simpson - Infamous for his pranks and kamikaze ways. Bart is the poster child for the ADHD personality. Per Wikipedia, Bart's hobbies include skateboarding, watching television (especially The Krusty the Clown Show which includes The Itchy & Scratchy Show), reading comic books (especially Radioactive Man), playing video games and generally causing mischief. Bart's rebellious attitude has made him a disruptive student at Springfield Elementary School, where Bart is an underachiever and proud of it.....in "Brother's Little Helper", (season eleven, 1999) it is revealed that Bart suffers from attention deficit disorder. "No Way Man!"

FINISH!

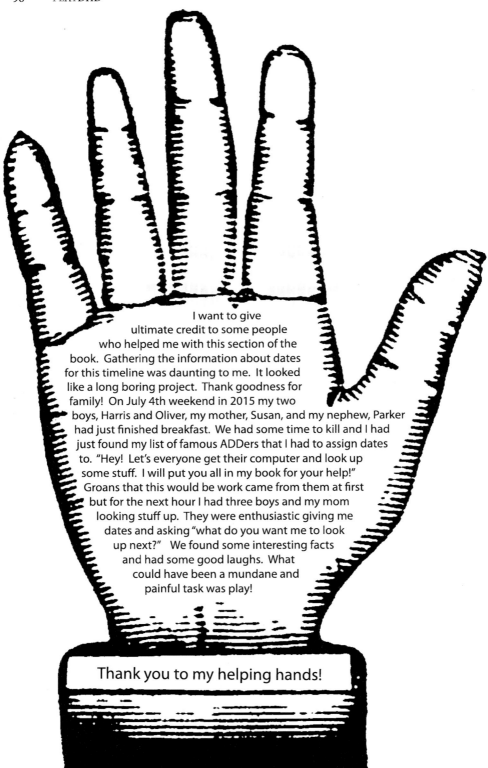

I want to give
ultimate credit to some people
who helped me with this section of the
book. Gathering the information about dates
for this timeline was daunting to me. It looked
like a long boring project. Thank goodness for
family! On July 4th weekend in 2015 my two
boys, Harris and Oliver, my mother, Susan, and my nephew, Parker
had just finished breakfast. We had some time to kill and I had
just found my list of famous ADDers that I had to assign dates
to. "Hey! Let's everyone get their computer and look up
some stuff. I will put you all in my book for your help!"
Groans that this would be work came from them at first
but for the next hour I had three boys and my mom
looking stuff up. They were enthusiastic giving me
dates and asking "what do you want me to look
up next?" We found some interesting facts
and had some good laughs. What
could have been a mundane and
painful task was play!

Thank you to my helping hands!

CHAPTER 5

READY, SET... PLAY!

One of my secrets to writing this book is that I hired a project manager/book coach, Jeff Zupancic. He's awesome! Except that when it came to this section he suggested that I give you "the formula" for how to be more playful. Here's the problem with that—there is no one way that works for everyone, no formula. It depends on how you "work," how you play, what motivates you, your support system, your mood, whether you were born under Jupiter rising... you get the picture. If you listen to Jeff Copper on Attention Talk Radio—if you don't, you should check out attentiontalkradio.com—you will often hear him say, "There is no top ten list that works for everyone." It's about knowing yourself and what works for you. (Apparently, what works for me is getting advice from guys named Jeff.)

What I offer you in this section is a few ways—okay, lots of ways—to be more playful. Do what works for you, depending on who you are, how you operate, and what your intuition tells you right now. Maybe next week you will want to try another strategy. And maybe you will come up with your own way to play. One thing I know about ADHD is that just because something interests you today doesn't mean it will be as compelling next week or ever again! Having options at hand or in mind is important.

Winging it

Playing around, winging it, being spontaneous, not making any plans, and, in dire times, procrastinating! Sometimes play is not going to be on your itinerary, but yet it is exactly what is needed. You might be sitting at your desk with writer's block—I've definitely been there—and no matter how long you sit and stare at the screen nothing comes to mind or you just can't seem to make yourself get in the mood to work. You can keep sitting there and hoping that the heavens will open and inspiration will part the clouds and land on you in your moment of need. More likely, especially if you have ADHD—which at this point we have established is probably an issue for you—the longer you sit there the harder it feels to think, much less stay awake. Your brain is shut-ting offffffffff... click! How do you turn it back on? Duh! Play! Get up. Do something! Move, talk, create... do something fun. Get away from your desk.

Someone told me that even in a situation like the one I just mentioned, playing felt like procrastination. Okay! But it's productive procrastination. You are putting off sitting unproductively in favor of doing something that will activate your brain so that you can come back and be productive. How can that be a bad thing? If you can't think about it from a scientific standpoint, you may have to just do it and see if it works for you.

---

productive procrastination.
noun
: Doing stuff to keep busy while avoiding what really needs doing.
: When all is said and done, your room is clean, your laundry is folded—but you haven't started your English paper.

(Thank urbandictionary.com for this forgiving concept.)

If you still feel guilty, set a timer while you play. See how long it takes to get in the mood to get back to productive work. Keep in mind that if you don't get back to work, perhaps you would have been unproductive anyway, whether you played or not. But at least you had some fun!

Use a timer as part of your play. Create a playful task, such as seeing how many nonsense words you can create in two minutes. Or stay a little closer to the writing project that has you stumped and brainstorm adjectives for two minutes. You're not even completely off-task, and you're amused, being goofy, and unclogging that writer's block.

Winging it is also a great strategy for those of you who just aren't ready to commit to this idea of habitually being playful. When opportunity presents itself, go for it. I suggest that you at least make an intention to evaluate the effect that being playful has on your mood, relationships, and productivity. Don't let the opportunity pass you by to recognize how play affects you and your symptoms of ADHD. While you are at it, notice how your playfulness affects people around you.

Take a lesson from Charlie Todd of Improv Everywhere (improveverywhere.com). He started his playful movement on a whim. He was working in an office job and was tasked with removing all the old phones. Charlie decided that he wanted to amuse himself and other people and so took one of the old corded office phones and strapped it to his belt and walked down the street pretending it was a cell phone. Mind you, this was 2001 and cell phones were already pretty mainstream items. Charlie did this just to see people's reactions and, I suspect, to amuse himself! Since then he has developed No Pants Day on the New York Subway system and numerous other community improv activities, just for fun. This started on a whim but became a habit eventually -- even a "prank collective."

Your Playlist

You want to take it a step further? How about having a PLAYbook of activities to choose from when you find yourself with some need or urge to play? Rather than winging it, if you have a menu you can quickly decide on what type of fun activity will fit the bill. If you have only 10 minutes of free time to play, you don't want to waste it trying to figure out what would be fun. Or if you have a free night, it's good to have a list of go-to activities or resources to create some spontaneous memories. Face it, when you have a moment of free time, you are likely to go to whatever activity is quick, easy, and familiar. This can mean a game on your phone, surfing the Internet, or watching a mindless TV show. If you are not in the habit of playing, having a list or a starting point already in front of you increases the likelihood that you will do something intentionally playful. You'll be glad you did.

How you organize the list is up to you: one long list; a list according to the amount of time you have; a list of nearby fun activities; lists of things you can do alone or with other people; or a list according to how much fun you want to have and how crazy you want to act.

Where do you put the list? I suggest somewhere so you always have it with you. For most people, that means their phone. But a tablet or a small notebook works too. I actually have a running note in my phone that has a list of fun activities I can refer to any time. On certain days of the week I receive notifications of upcoming events in my area that might be fun, and I put these in a separate task folder right in my calendar app. That way if Saturday rolls around and I want something new to do I can look at local events I thought I might be interested in and I'm off to have some fun!

You're curious what my
playlist looks like?
I thought you'd never ask!

Kirsten's Playlist

Concert at any venue
Go to music store and play drums
Trampoline in the backyard
Trampoline Park
Bowling
Walk on the beach
Walk the dogs
Board game with kids
Trivia Crack (an online game I enjoy)
Play ball with the dogs
Bring the dogs to the dog park
Shopping!
Go on a date
Dress up in a hat
Wear a favorite item of clothing
Go for a drive without the GPS (get lost)
Snow tubing (winter only)
Try a new restaurant
Go on a "date" with one or both of my kids
Target shooting
Color in my coloring book
Volunteer
Have sex
Call a long-lost friend
Go on a weekend getaway
Make something
Bike ride
Horseback riding
Go to a play

Window shop/try on clothes I would never buy or can't afford
Test drive a sports car
Have a party!
Go for a walk in the woods
Finger painting
Lie in the hammock
Go to the park and get on a swing
Museum of Science
Sledding
Slumber party
Compliment someone
Dance
Bake
Take a class
Hula hoop
Take a trip

If you're still a little stuck on what to put on your playlist, here are some great places to start:

1. Take into account your Play Personality (from Chapter 4. If you are a kinesthetic and enjoy movement or sports, include some physical activities. If you are a Competitor, include more challenging activities. If you're a Performer, your list might include practicing or playing a new instrument or participating in an improv group. Since most people have aspects of more than one play personality, your list should also reflect your diverse interests.

2. Go back to your play history (Chapter 4, in case you skipped ahead) and remember some of the ways you have enjoyed playing over the course of your life. If you are someone who likes playing alone, consider this when you make your list. If, like me, you have enjoyed dressing up as part of your play, include dressing in your most fabulous hat, your funkiest shirt, or something else that makes you feel playful during the day.

3. Obviously, you should include anything that comes to mind or presents itself that just sounds like it would be fun. Riding the subway without pants for No Pants Day may not be your idea of fun, but being on the subway to see other people do so may be just the laugh you need! Put it on the list!

Michael Tertes (michaeltertes.com) shared his idea of an "Alive List." This is what he suggests:

"Keep a list of any activity that makes you feel alive... energized, optimistic, satisfied, hopeful, fulfilled, full of possibility and potential. Make sure to include activities that may initially be uncomfortable and yet leave you feeling more alive. Review this list regularly and explore how you can incorporate more of these activities into your life. Also, look for themes and how to incorporate those themes into your life. Simply the act of tracking them in this way can have a surprisingly positive impact."

The BAP (Big Audacious Play)

We use structure to make sure we accomplish all of the "hard stuff," and when we finally have time off we "wing it." Now I am all for improvising, spontaneity, and acting in the moment, but often times we go to our default activities—checking email, watching television, surfing the internet, getting coffee, or calling a friend. There's nothing wrong with these things. But why not plan to do something new? Something a little more exciting, more memorable, more stimulating? Try a new restaurant, meet someone new, go back to an old hobby you put away long ago, take a walk somewhere you haven't gone before, explore, be curious. Or simply do something you already enjoy--but do it differently.

OKAY, STOP! Don't read this chapter if you are not ready to actually make plans and commit to being playful!

This is actually a test to see how ADHD you are! When you have ADHD, being told what to do is often taken as an opportunity to be a rebel or take on a challenge. For instance, when I was in high school, my math and science teachers both advised me to pursue their respective subjects in college. My psychology teacher, however, said, "Kirsten, whatever you do, don't go into psychology." In that moment I knew exactly what I would be when I grew up! I enrolled in college as a psychology major and never wavered. You know I took that as a powerful challenge because it kept me focused on a goal for eight years!

Don't get scared off by my use of the word "big." Your plan may be a "relatively" big plan. If you start from being an extremely serious, hard-working person who is still having some doubts about how effective being playful might be, having a "big" plan can mean crafting a short list of ways to be more playful while staying in your cubicle. For those of you who tend to have an "all or nothing" approach to trying new things, your plan may be a bit more audacious. Take it at whatever pace feels appropriate. We can all have a tendency to jump in the deep end only to find the water is too cold, and then we want to get out as fast as we can and never get back in. So, go at your own pace. Try some things. If they don't work, do it differently. There are—metaphorically speaking—so many pools to play in. Some are bigger and deeper than others. Find your plan to play that is just right so you can sustain it and build on this habit.

One of the ways I get my clients to follow through on goals is to emphasize the importance of getting the idea out of their head and onto paper. I use the quote from the famous Dr. Milliken (which would be me): "It's not real until it's written."

People with ADHD are generally brilliant. But we fool ourselves into believing that this should mean we have a great working memory. How many times have you told yourself that you'll remember without writing something down? And how many times have you forgotten? I used to do this a lot! How many great ideas for inventions did I miss out on because I didn't write it down and someone else did?

When you are honest with yourself you will admit that recording your thoughts is probably a better strategy than "trying" to remember. You don't lose points for writing things down. In fact, people will be impressed by your ability to "remember" your commitments and your ideas.

In creating a plan to play, you now have one more thing to keep track of. When do you have time to play? Or, what time do you want to reserve for play (how's that for high-level planning)? I too started with "winging it" when I decided I wanted to be more playful. As I began seeing how useful play was and how much better life was when I incorporated play time in my life, I wanted to be more intentional about scheduling this time. I already had a calendar for keeping myself organized and managing my business appointments. Instead of reinventing the wheel, I created a new tag and color for my play "appointments" and began inserting them into my calendar. By making them look different from my business commitments, I could visualize when my next play time was.

Today, most people have some form of online calendar. If you have developed a habit of looking at an online calendar on a regular (at least daily) basis, use this to record your plans to play. A paper calendar works, too, and has more doodle-ability, if doodling is one of your playful joys. I use both electronic and paper planners. When I use paper, I gravitate toward colors and designs that appeal to me, something with a pretty cover that I can put in my bag. I like to plan my day in 15-minute increments, and I want the slots to be big enough to actually write in without a magnifying glass. I also like having space for notes and doodles. I carry various pens so that the page looks visually interesting. You might want to color code your appointments the way my friend Darcy does (personally, I can't keep track of that sort of color legend or carry enough pens). You may go through several different calendars before you find one that you really love. Choose a size, layout, and design that you feel will work for you. Think about how you like to record your notes and appointments. You may also want to consider the writing instrument you will use to do this. Some pens are simply more fun than others.

If you use an electronic calendar you often have the option to set this up to look and perform in a way that suits you best. I use Pocket Informant (http://pocketinformant.com/) and Google calendar. I also have an online scheduling tool (scheduleonce.com) so people can schedule time to work (or play) with me. Of course, if you use more than one tool you'll want to be sure they all sync. I check just one calendar on my phone. My calendar app also lets me keep a running playlist of upcoming or regular fun activities that I may want to schedule or simply do on the spur of the moment.

So how do you use a calendar to plan to play? This may challenge your sensibility about scheduling. But just stay with me through the next bit.

If, then… Do you ever find yourself negotiating either out loud or privately for play time? If I just finish this report, then I will give myself time to play. What if it were the other way around? If I play for 15 minutes, then I will be giving myself the mental capacity to work more productively, be more creative, and feel more focused on my work.

You still with me? What do you think of making play the priority? It's like a restaurant near my home that has the slogan "Eat Dessert First." Why stuff yourself to have a treat after your meal? Eat the treat first! When I was a kid, my grandmother used to say that if we ate all our breakfast we could have ice cream (dessert with breakfast). Of course, breakfast was a sugary cereal and donuts! What an amazing grandma!

- When we apply the idea of "dessert first" to scheduling play, it looks like this:

- Make a list of all the fun and playful things you regularly do in a week and about how much time you need for each activity. Think about the shows you enjoy watching, the activities you attend regularly, and the little things you do that give you joy. Depending on your feeling about some of these things, you might include going to the gym, playing on a team, attending classes, date night, massage appointments, and so on—things that happen on a regular and predictable basis. While this might be a short list for now, as you continue practicing the habit of being playful this list will likely grow.

- Make a list each week or month of things that are going on that are special. Again, estimate how much time you need for each— and include travel or preparation time. Special stuff might include concerts, visiting with a friend, getting your hair cut (one of my favorites), traveling, and other events that you do once in a while.

- The final list is your "have to-dos." This might include "work," getting your car fixed, doing laundry, or cleaning the house (believe it or not, I have a friend who puts this under regular fun!). Some of these events might be vague, especially if you work for someone else. You know you have to work a certain number of hours or have a particular project you are working on. You can break these down into more specific smaller chunks or tasks when you write them in the calendar. For instance, one of my to-dos is often "writing." This gets more specific as the time gets closer and I might write in "write blog post on 'playing with the truth.'"

- Now the real challenge—using your calendar.

- Start with list 1—fun things you do on a regular basis. Fill these into your schedule first. You may want to do this in pencil or erasable pen. Trust me here. If you are focusing on developing a more playful mindset you have to make play a priority. This will bleed into your "have to-dos" as you practice more.

- Fill in the events from list 2—special fun events.

- I know you can see the pattern here.... Now fill in the "have to dos" from list 3.

There may be conflicts with some of your play appointments. This is where you have to negotiate and compromise. There are no hard and fast rules here. The more committed to being playful you are, the more flexibility you have in your work life, and the more you can integrate fun and play into your "have to do" activities, the less you have to compromise and the more productive you will become.

That said, your calendar does not care—tell a friend!

I love using calendars to commit to a plan, remind myself of an appointment, and plan my intentions to get things done. But there are times when I have things written down, have the best of intentions, and end up sitting on the couch doing nothing! There are no obvious repercussions, especially if what was planned doesn't involve another person. If I didn't keep my plans to write each chapter of my book no one suffered and no one cared in that moment. But I lost an opportunity to make progress.

How often do you say you want to do something for yourself or to better yourself but end up blowing it off? How often does that happen when you have plans with another person or an appointment with someone you care about? Not nearly as often, right? When you are starting a new routine, having someone else to join you makes you a million times more likely to stick to the plan (I can't put my finger on the study that I got this number from, but I swear I read it somewhere). For instance, if you intend to start a new habit of going to the gym, you are more likely to start and persevere if you have a workout buddy. I can't tell you how many times I woke at 5 a.m. to go to the gym and wanted to go back to sleep. But I didn't because I didn't want to let my friends down.

As you begin this journey to becoming more playful, find people to play with. Make plans that will be fun. Heck, I even find that work is more fun when I have someone else sitting in the same space as me, because we can schedule breaks together and have moments of playful conversation and fun to re-infuse energy and playfulness into our work. As you put aside time in your calendar for play appointments, include names of people you've made plans with. Even if they forget that you talked about going to a free concert together, you can check in with them again the day before. Remember, people are impressed by your memory skills when you write stuff down.

Outside In

Likely you have heard someone say "Fake it till you make it." If you feel like crap, smile until you feel happy. If you feel depressed, "act" playful until you feel that way. Sometimes it may help to have a little prompt or prop to get you started. Surrounding yourself with colors, images, and objects that make you feel energized and happy and trigger a smile can get the "juices" (dopamine) flowing and make it easier to feel playful.

Some days the stresses of life can make you feel anything but playful. This, in turn, can make everything feel difficult. Problem solving seems impossible. The day becomes something to just get through rather than providing opportunities for enjoyment. Gratitude is far from your mind. Staying in this frame of mind is not productive, and it just doesn't feel good. Getting out of this mindset can feel like an enormous, if not impossible, task. Planning ahead by setting up your environment and having props that can jump-start your "funny bone" can make it easier.

I have certain clothes that I save that make me feel particularly happy and playful when I wear them. I also have an awesome hat collection—both new and vintage—that instantly makes me happy, and other people smile or give me compliments, which also makes me happy. I find that when someone compliments me or when I give a compliment I can't help but feel joyful. Perhaps dressing up is not your thing. There are many ways to create an environment that can help you feel on your way to being more playful.

What makes you smile when you see it? A picture of someone you love? A flowering plant? A painting? Your cats playing? Are there colors that make you feel happy and energized? Patterns that convey playfulness for you?

What type of sound do you associate with playfulness? Hip-hop? A dramatic classical piece? The sound of other people giggling? The Song "Adults Doing the Happy Dance (ADHD)"? (Yes, this is a real song written by Harold Payne. Google it!)

What makes you feel happy when you hold it? A Koosh ball? A fidget toy? An Etch-A-Sketch? Thinking Putty? A puppy (who doesn't love holding a puppy?!)?

On my path to being more playful, I started off slowly. Going to the office supply store was actually my first effort at incorporating more playfulness in my work day. I bought fun file folders, binders in bright colors, and lots of colored pens and hi-liters. I probably have the largest collection of sticky notes in the universe outside an office supply store!

Eventually, I graduated from the office supply store to the toy store, where I found fidget toys and other manipulatives, origami paper, puzzles, and classic games. I got into collecting magnet figures and finding places to stick them all around my office and home.

Next, I got playful with paint, choosing new colors for my walls. I often painted just one wall in a room with a bright color. Some of them also got funky patterns or art work applied.

Once I had the visual and tactile addressed, I started investing some money into seating and standing options. I love my standing work desks (yes, I have more than one). To have the option to sit while working, I also bought tall wobble stools. I am not a big fan of chairs. So I invested in bean bag chairs (Yogibos, to be specific). These are the best because I can adjust to sit up, recline, or lie down. Furniture that was "Fun-ctional" proved to be a worthwhile investment. I feel more energized and playful when I am comfortable and can move around, whether I am working or having fun—or working and having fun.

For a relatively small cost, I found a carpet company (FLOR.com) that makes floor tiles that I had made into a hopscotch board, a putting green, and a 5-foot-square chess/checker board.

Finally, I splurged on a 14-foot trampoline. And my boys and I are working on plans for a treehouse.

What are things that make you happy? Make a list to remind yourself of images, sounds, and things that make you happy. Keep this somewhere so that you can pull it out and remind yourself when you need a reminder of how to get happy.

Get started with a list of 5 things—and add to it as more come to mind.

1. _____
   _____
   _____

2. _____
   _____
   _____

3. _____
   _____
   _____

4. _____
   _____
   _____

5. _____
   _____
   _____

Or more. _____
   _____
   _____
   _____
   _____
   _____
   _____
   _____
   _____

Playing Well with Others

So far we have been mostly talking about going it on your own. Some of you will naturally seek out other people to play with. Others tend to be shy, reserved and perhaps more internal in their forms of play. Chapter 3 addressed elements that support developing new habits. Belief in your ability to adopt a new habit is important. And having belief in yourself can be powerfully influenced by being part of a group. It's also true that when we commit to others our intention to adopt a habit, we are more likely to follow through than when we keep our plans to ourselves.

In other words, friends and acquaintances who like to play are important.

Are you a leader or a follower? Both are important roles. But if you are a leader you may be the one instigating the playfulness. If you are a follower, you want to find others who are already playing so you can join in. When you are in the process of strengthening your playful habit it is sometimes easier to be a follower for a bit until your funny bone has had a chance to get loose again. Then it can be fun to take the reins and coax your friends into joining in your ideas for fun!

People are attracted to others who are happy and playful. Some people might just watch and smile, while others will feel the undeniable urge to join in. No matter what, playfulness is infectious. Finding a playmate—not THAT kind—is likely to be easier than you imagine. When you were a kid, simply asking "Do you want to play?" was a good enough invitation to fun. Why not use the same strategy as an adult? Just ask!

Okay, adults have some hang-ups about the idea of "playing". I know this is probably not news to you. But you have to be prepared for the fact that other people are not as enlightened as you about the powerful effects of being playful. You may have to rephrase the invitation, "Do you want to have some fun?" Even with this you may still experience rejection. Nobody says, "Fun? No, sorry, I don't like fun." But your idea of fun and their idea of fun might not match up. It's important to meet people where they are at.

Choose your playmates by paying attention to body language and facial expressions. That lady sitting on the park bench with a scowl on her face may not be receptive to your invitation. But the guy sitting on the edge of his seat with a big smile on his face may be ready to jump up and join in.

You may have to "show" them how to be playful before they will join in. There are some easy ways to get adults to play. For instance, tell a joke. Adults love jokes. Once someone tells a joke, it typically inspires others to share a joke themselves. Voila! Playfulness! You can leave it at that or use the momentum to get people to join you in another form of fun.

Some more ideas to get you playing with others:

- Join a group of like-minded people. Again, take into consideration your play personality and your play history. How do you like to play, and who else is playing like that? You could join a local softball league, take an art class, or learn to sail. Local adult education and recreation departments can introduce you to all sorts of hobbies. I once took a six-week hula hooping class through my local adult education/recreation program. It was a blast!

- Find a playmate. Again, not necessarily THAT kind (but those are good too). We're talking about someone who wants to try or do some of the same things you are interested in. I actually put ads in local venues (i.e., dating sites) saying I am looking for someone to go sky diving with me this summer. I had a running partner for a while that I found through Craigslist. Over the winter I was looking for a playmate to learn to snowboard with me. That was fun—and painful! Craigslist. com has a section to find activity buddies in your community.

- Plan some fun and send out an E-vite to your friends and Facebook family. Have you always wanted to learn to do Stand-Up Paddleboarding (SUP) but don't want to be the only one on the water? Invite everyone you know to a SUP party. Or maybe you want to get involved in a local fundraising event with your own team. If you are really crafty, you can send actual invitations in the mail and make that part of your fun. I plan at least one party a year and invite everyone I know. I am always surprised that at least one or two friends from out of town make a plan to come to the celebration. By adding the promise of fun, games, or an interesting activity people seem more inclined to make the effort to join me.

- Join a local Meetup group (Meetup.com). I have attended meetups focused on business networking, ghost hunting (I never saw one), running, and the Law of Attraction. Attending was not always about my passion for the group topic but about who I thought would be there. I have had a lot of fun and made a lot of friends through attending meetups.

- Join an adult ADHD support group. While not every community has one, if you can find a group of adults with ADHD to chat, socialize, learn, and have fun with you will have fun. When I was running an adult ADHD group it was always filled with playfulness. In fact, rather than sit around we often had some kind of activity involved. When I have something in common with people in a group, I'm more inclined to be myself and be playful.

If you really want to have fun, attend an ADHD conference. It's heaven! I still remember the first time I attended an ADHD Coaches Conference. I was nervous and then mortified when I blurted something semi-idiotic out to someone I was trying to impress. I realized ten minutes later that no one commented nor even cared. Everyone was blurting! It was acceptable and expected. I was able to have the most fun ever because I was not constantly worried about just being myself.

Kidding Around

It's been said that the real reason we have kids is to be able to play again—and not just the playing that resulted in conception. Kids are just better at play.

This past summer I attended a class on the joy of play at a retreat center in upstate New York. I hadn't realized that this was taking place during Family Week, so my kids were not with me. The other thirty adults in the class had kids attending other programs at the camp. I was repeatedly asked if it was uncomfortable for me having so many kids around. "No!" I said, "It's perfect! They are the best role models for play!" Our adult group raided them and they raided us in an exponentially better way. I made more friends—both kids and adults—in one week because we were all focused on play together. I can't wait to go back next summer with my own kids in tow!

One of the joys of being a parent is the opportunity to play with our kids. On the other hand, one of the stresses of being a parent is trusting our kids to direct their own play. They might get hurt or hurt someone else physically or emotionally. If your child has inherited your ADHD they might be hyperactive, impulsive, not pick up on social cues, or be awkward interacting in groups. If you struggle with parenting a child with ADHD, I strongly suggest that you contact the amazing team at ImpactADHD (www.impactadhd.com). They help parents of kids with ADHD negotiate everything from dealing with the school system to talking with medical providers and playing with your kids.

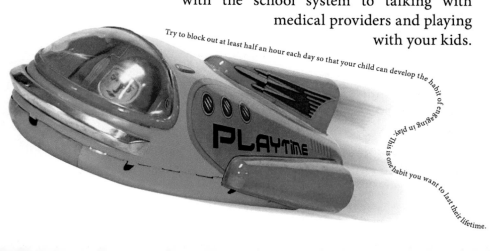

Try to block out at least half an hour each day so that your child can develop the habit of engaging in play. This is one habit you want to last their lifetime.

This following section addresses being an adult with ADHD and playing with your own child or children—or someone else's, if you have permission.

First, consider the child's play personality (refer back to Chapter 4). Remember that just because you are related doesn't mean your child will necessarily have the same play personality as you do! As the grown-up you may have to have fun the way your child prefers or find ways to meet both your interests. For instance, your child may be an Explorer and you may be more of an Artist type. Finding common interest by telling a story about an adventure you imagine having together and then depicting the story through painting, building, or collages may hold interest for both of you.

Do you remember playing Follow the Leader when you were young? Did you like being a follower? I didn't. It was easier to be the leader. I could make the rules and it felt good to have other people following my orders (yes, I tend to be bossy!). But, as a parent, it's important to be a good follower. Let your daughter be the leader, and she'll see that you trust her. Let her make mistakes, help her recover and try again. It's important for adults to resist the urge to lead and instead to follow their child wherever their imagination leads (within reason). GET OUT OF THE WAY AND LET THEM PLAY! The bonus is that we can let go of control, enjoy the moment, and be in for some amazing surprises and fun when we learn to follow a small leader.

Here is a challenge. I dare you to have a "say yes" day with your child. Anything they suggest you have to say "yes" to—within reason, of course, but be lenient.

Imaginary play and free play are the ideal forms of play for both fun and building executive function skills such as self-control, social skills, and working memory. Putting on a play, creating a story, playing dress-up, playing with dolls or cars, or playing house are all forms of imaginary play. Free play can include rough-and-tumble play, running around aimlessly, climbing trees, or hanging upside down at the playground, seeing the world from another perspective.

Likewise, researchers are finding that playing in nature also reduces symptoms of ADHD for both kids and adults. Playing in green outdoor settings is thought to reduce attention fatigue. The reasons for this are not clear. It can't be coincidence that many guided imagery scripts use outdoor settings as the focus for helping people relax. A walk on the beach, jumping in a lake, finding a path in the forest, or going for a long hike up a mountain are activities that are simultaneously relaxing and invigorating—and can be done as a family.

Physical activity is important for brain development and improving symptoms of ADHD at any age. Playing sports, riding bikes, running, swimming, karate, tag, soccer, horseback riding, and other outdoor pursuits are fun activities that you can join in, coach, or watch from the sidelines with your child. If you are stuck inside, you might consider building your own obstacle course out of hula hoops, pillows, beanbag chairs, jump ropes, and other objects around the house. Engage your child in conceptualizing and building the course.

Play can take any form. Cooking can be playful. Cleaning the house can be playful (if done right). Heck, I make a game out of cleaning up dog poop! Mind you, some activities are inherently more playful than others. There are games you can play while driving in the car (hangman or I Spy). You can build a sand castle on the beach or in a sand box. Plant a garden in your backyard or a window box. Ride your bike and find a new area to explore or imagine going somewhere and tell a story about it that you make up together. There are a million ways to play (probably more like a gazillion ways).

Don't worry about whether you are choosing activities that will target specific symptoms of ADHD. Ultimately, the purpose of play is for both of you to have fun!

CHAPTER 6
LET'S TALK ABOUT SEX

There, I got your attention, didn't I? "Sex is the playground of adults," says psychologist Dr. Ari Tuckman (I love this quote so much, I used it twice in this book!). But it doesn't start with the physical act of making love. Everything leading up to sex can—and should—involve play as well. There is interest, motivation, challenge, risk, rules, incentives, and fun! And you want to keep doing it. Courtship is like one big game. Who calls who? How long do you wait to call after the date? What do you do to keep the other person interested? When can you "score"? (Have you ever noticed that we talk about sex in terms of America's favorite game—baseball! Getting to the bases—what is third base but sex?)

Sex is one of the most fun, most playful activities consenting adults can indulge in together. Get the un-fun but oh-so-important talk about safe sex, STD status and birth control out of the way and let the games begin. Just like with any other sort of play, be sure to set aside time and make it a priority. And, just like with any sort of play, novelty can be the key to keeping you, um, interested.

And yes, there is an app for that! There is an app (at the time I am writing this) called "Spreadsheets." The app gamifies sex. Points, badges, levels, challenges. The app monitors your movement and decibel level during coitus (sex) and gives you challenges such as having morning sex to improve your stats. The only drawback to this app is that you have to "play" with a partner. There is no masturbation mode.

If you have not gone to your local sex shop, make a date of it. Even if you buy nothing, this is a great date—and probably a chance to learn something new about your partner. Peruse the videos, costumes, books, toys, and gadgets. If you are lucky enough to have a really good sex shop, they may offer classes. These usually involve clothes on, mature conversations, and matter-of-fact demonstrations. But, beware, some are a little more risqué!

Get Kinky—Or Not (Partner Play)

I once wrote an article for ADHD-challenged couples called "ADD-Adventure Deficit Disorder." The premise of the article was that while courtship is an ideal environment for someone with ADHD to shine, once the metaphorical honeymoon is over and the routines of day-to-day life become predominant, symptoms of ADHD can cause relationship problems. Therefore, making a point of having adventures, shaking things up a bit, and being playful can be crucial to the success of your relationship.

Boredom and lack of motivation are not just problems in the work setting. Just like a new job, a shiny new relationship is ideal for activating dopamine and turning on the old ADHD brain. Courtship is an ideal form of play. But most relationships eventually lose that sizzle, and the routines of daily life infiltrate the once-novel excitement of new love. Once the newness in a relationship is gone, we can have difficulty feeling inspired, excited, motivated, and creative. Knowing this about ourselves and letting our partner in on this dirty little secret can be the key to creating a plan to keep the spark ignited and the fun in the relationship for the long term.

So what do you do? Everything I have offered about being playful so far applies to your relationships just as it does every other area of your life. How do you bring your play personality to the relationship? How do you accommodate your partner's play personality in the fun you have together? If you have been in a relationship long enough for the sizzle to be barely a crackle, how do you create a new habit of being more playful and creating a roaring fire between you again? Here are some ideas to get you started.

I love a challenge—both giving challenges and being challenged. Date nights can be made fun by introducing dares to your partner.

I once dated a man who was somewhat shy in social situations. He described himself as "vanilla" when it came to his brand of fun. He took me out to dinner, during which I dared him to tell the manager that it was our 20th anniversary. He laughed and said there was "no way" he was going to do this. I continued to goad him and when the manager came to our table he chatted with him for a moment and then surprised me by saying, "I'm so happy we are here. It's our 20th anniversary tonight!" The manager immediately congratulated us and offered us a free round of drinks. I have to say this moment still makes me smile because my date was so not the guy to do something like that. I have also heard of couples telling hotels that they were on their honeymoon. The reaction of the staff adds to the excitement and can be the audience that you need to really act the part! A more common—but nonetheless fun—game is to role play as someone totally different than yourself. You can meet at a bar or start in the bedroom and play out your fantasy with your partner.

Finding a Playmate (Not that kind!)

Trying to meet someone? There are apps for learning to play the flirtation game and for practicing your moves on potential partners. There are apps called Flirt Planet Play and Flirt Planet Meet.

If you prefer to meet someone the old-fashioned way, you can use a great pick up line, you know, in person. I am going to share my favorite pick-up line. I have used this since I was eighteen years old. It never fails, and it works on women and men. Here it is... da, da, da…. "How's your goldfish?" Silly? Think about it. Most people have owned a goldfish or another type of fish, whether from a pet store or from one of those "get the ball in the bowl" games at a carnival. There is always a story to go with that experience. If not, that is a conversation in itself about how deprived they were as a kid. Try it. Trust me. It never fails.

Rules of meeting, flirting, dating, and relationships can be complicated or easy. It depends on the couple. Rules about who calls who, when you can call, how often it is appropriate to text. Do you communicate during the work day? From communication to contact… rules about touching in private and public. What boundaries do you each have in various areas of your life? These are all things to learn either by testing the waters or talking about them directly with your partner. They are different from person to person and relationship to relationship.

Moving into a relationship but still outside of the bedroom (or whatever room you have sex in), you can flirt via phone, email, text, or in person. Heck, I suppose you can also flirt via fax—as long as you know the intended party will be the only one to see your message. Text, stories, images, video—from an innocuous "I'm thinking about you" to something a bit more racy and specific like "10 pm tonight in the kitchen with the spatula!" And we're not talking about omelets!

How about a treasure hunt? Hiding romantic gifts and giving your partner a treasure map to find them. Perhaps you are the last treasure to be found!

CHAPTER 7

GAMIFY ANYTHING

I wanted to name this chapter "Bored Games." When I am faced with a task that I particularly do not like, I feel bored. Just like the teenagers and kids I interview will describe their least favorite or most difficult subject in school as "boring." What they are really telling me is that they have no interest or motivation to engage in the subject so it feels HARD! When things are hard the brain effectively is in the "off" position. So how do you turn it "on"? Turn the task into a game. Thank goodness we live in a time when "gamification" is an actual thing.

Gamification is the use of game design elements in non-game context. So how do you take a task that is typically considered "not a game" and turn it into a game? Think like a game designer. Think of your favorite game. What makes it fun? What keeps you wanting to play? Games typically involve clear rules and goals, a level of risk, constant feedback or rewards, challenge, and momentum. They are voluntary and involve a sense of fun.

- Goals provide a way to keep score and to determine who wins.
- Rules keep things predictable and consistent.
- Having a level of risk makes the "player" consider their strategy for playing and keeps them focused.
- Feedback provides encouragement and lets the player assess their progress and strategy.
- It's important that the level of challenge keeps the player interested by not being too easy, but not overwhelmed by being too hard.
- Rewards are frequent and provide immediate gratification to keep the player motivated to continue. Rewards can include verbal feedback, badges, points, "leveling up," increased status, immunity, currency, and loot.
- Fun keeps the player smiling and is an indication of the intrinsic (internal) reward involved in playing a satisfying game.

Using these pointers, you can start to "gamify" those hard-to-do, much avoided, often procrastinated, head-banging tasks you have been putting off at home and work. Or you can get your kids to do them!

Gamifying Dreaded Tasks

Assign a point system to everything you don't enjoy (sucky tasks) and rewards you can enjoy (happiness). The harder the task (this is subjective) the higher the point value. Likewise, the more you like a reward the higher the point value. The concept is that you have to accrue enough sucky task points to buy a reward.
To get started make two lists: one of the sucky tasks and the other of your rewards. Then assign point values. You may have to tweak these as you go along. Keep track of points and identify the rewards you are "playing" for.

Here's a quick and dirty example:

SUCKY TASK	REWARD
Load of laundry, 3 points	Trampoline Park, 10 points
Clean Bathroom, 5 points	Go out for dessert, 15 points
Dreaded email, 2 points	Buy new hat, 30 points
Clean yard, 6 points	Disney World, 300 points

For instance, if you want to go to the Trampoline Park, you need to earn 10 points. This might involve having to do the laundry (1 load = 3 points), clean the bathroom (5 points), and reply to that email from your boss that you have been putting off (2 points).

When you are working on big goals or long-term projects, you can gamify your progress by breaking down the goal into bite-sized chunks that can be done in short spurts. Set milestones for yourself and each time you complete one, reward yourself. Have a system to visualize and track your progress. For example, if you want to plan a trip to Disney World as a family, you can gamify and track everything it takes to prepare for the trip. You have to save money, plan activities, and make reservations.

I personally like the challenge of racing against time. This can involve timing myself and trying to beat my own time on tasks; racing another person to see who can get their task done the quickest (without errors); or setting a time limit and seeing how many tasks I can get done in a set time. Whenever I am driving somewhere, I like to call ahead and give an exact time when I will arrive. I have been doing this since before GPS told me when I should arrive. It's a little game to see how close to that time I actually arrive. There is something about the pressure of short periods of time that is invigorating. I'm sure it is related to my affinity for procrastinating until the very last possible moment on a task.

There's an App for That

There are many other apps and online platforms to gamify even the most dreaded activity.

- For me, household chores are a dreaded activity. That is, until I discovered CHOREWARS! (www.chorewars.com/). Chore Wars turns doing the dishes, vacuuming the floor, taking out the trash, and doing the laundry into a game for the whole family! As you progress, you'll randomly encounter monsters, pick up dropped loot and gold, unlock treasure, and improve your character. The "dungeon master" can assign new quests and challenge the party with something new. When you encounter monsters, your HP (health points -- I had to ask one of my kids about that one!) and character progression comes into play—you'll actually fight the monster, and how well you've built up your character to this point will make a difference, so there's incentive to actually do the chores.

- Running is also not my favorite thing to do unless my attention is distracted by something else. Good music is one way to keep me going. There are also apps, such as Zombie Run (a story) or Couch to 5K (verbal encouragement and time markers). If having a community behind you in your quest for health is motivating, Fitocracy might work for you.

- Have a long to-do list? Apps like Epic Win gamify getting done your "to-dos." Want to develop better habits? HabitRPG turns better behavior into a game of survival. As you get things done, you'll gain levels, which unlock more features. When you miss your to-dos, your health takes a hit, and if you miss too many things on your to-do list, your stats begin to take a hit and you lose momentum toward the next level or set of bonuses you were aiming for.

- Well-known game designer Jane McGonigal developed SuperBetter to help people tackle one challenge at a time. SuperBetter breaks down your goal into a journey to be a better you—with all the trials, challenges, and setbacks that come with trying to make a major change.

Need an app for some other sucky task? Search the web for "gamify anything."

CHAPTER 8

YOUR PERSONAL PLAYLIST

This is what we've all been waiting for—lists of ways to play. These lists are a conglomeration of ideas I found online, many conversations during snack time at Peloton Labs (a co-working space in Portland, Maine), conversations with random strangers, and conversations with even stranger friends. It also includes a number of ideas from my kids and from my very own imagination!

Although these lists are divided into categories, these are very "loose." Adults can certainly play together in activities from the kids' play list. You also don't have to be in a formal work setting (or any work setting) to use some of the ideas from the list to make work more playful. Okay, I would not suggest that you do most of the items on the parent play list when you are playing as a parent with your child. Other than that, feel free to grab ideas from any list anytime.

---

6 impossible things before breakfast.

"One can't believe impossible things."

"I daresay you haven't had much practice," said the Queen. "When I was your age, I always did it for half-an-hour a day. Why, sometimes I've believed as many as six impossible things before breakfast."

—*Alice In Wonderland, Lewis Carroll*

These are not checklists; they're ideas to get you going. Find some that resonate for you, some that cause you to pause and imagine what it would be like to do them. Find one or more that makes you smile. Then decide how and when you will use the idea— take it verbatim, change it, or generate a whole new idea from it. Put it in your calendar. Call someone and ask them to join you. Whatever you do—play!

CHAPTER 8 - YOUR PERSONAL PLAYLIST   127

Everyday Life (Anywhere, with Anyone or No One at All)

- Use the basic rules of improv. By its very nature, improvisation (improv) is playful.
  1. Before saying "no," ask "why not?" and "what's possible?"
  2. Say "yes," and if you get really good at that you can say "yes, and…"
  3. There are no mistakes, only opportunities.
  4. Make the other person look good.
- Move.
- Smile more.
- Tell a joke or laugh at someone else's joke.
- See how long you can hold your breath.
- Spend time around young children.
- Play with young, active dogs.
- Do art without thought of success.
- Say hello to people you don't know, or give a random stranger a compliment

CONVERSATION STARTERS: "FLYING OR INVISIBILITY?"

- Get a couple of different magnetic poetry kits and combine them.
- Watch silly cat videos on YouTube.
- Online challenge games like Words With Friends or Trivia Crack.
- Dance.
- Invite a few fun friends over for a "play date."
- Host a regular game night with friends.
- Schedule time at the beach or in a park to throw a Frisbee or fly a kite with friends.
- Joke with strangers at a bus stop or in a checkout line. It'll make the time pass quicker.
- Visit a magic store and learn some tricks. Or invest in art supplies, construction toys, or science kits and create something new.
- Try new foods.

- Learn something new (take a painting class, or take up drumming and dancing to beats of a different culture).
- Take a walk or day trip without any plans or route—toss a coin to decide what direction you will go and don't keep track of your route. Just take in the scenery.
- Jump in puddles.
- Reorganize or rearrange your space.
- Call the adult education program and sign up for a class (and actually go!).

Make a **PLAN** for something **RANDOM** or out of the ordinary during the day. This gives you something to look forward to. In the middle of the day it can also help you to recharge.

Some people (not me) enjoy cleaning their space. The organization and productivity is fun to them (weird, right?). My friend Colby loves cleaning. I would invite her to my house when I needed to clean because I knew she loved this and because I knew that would make me start before she got there. Whether you love cleaning or not, turn on the music or "whistle while you work"!

- Smash watermelons, pumpkins, and chipped plates (wear safety goggles for fun and protection).
- Pose for pictures while hotel bed jumping.
- Let go of helium balloons. For maximum enjoyment, make sure there are kids present.
- Take a train ride.
- Hula hoop.
- Play hopscotch.
- Turn your sidewalk into an art gallery with sidewalk chalk.
- Wage a spit-ball war.
- Fly a kite.
- Explore alleys.
- Learn to make jam.
- Shop your pantry, and create a meal from your leftovers.
- Go outside, roll down a hill, climb a tree, or build a treehouse.

- Try something new, like surfing, snowboarding, jumping on a trampoline, or rock climbing.
- Go to Burning Man, the ultimate celebration of adult play.
- Travel to a new spot, near or far.
- Finger paint.
- Create a play persona. When you are stuck, put on an article of clothing, an accent to help change your mindset.
- Do things you're not supposed to do. Break the rules, make a scene, put on a show. Drive one of those little electric cart things around the grocery store. Wear your pajamas to work.
- Make something just because you can. A new piece of furniture, a treehouse, a song, or a birthday card for a close friend.
- Pet someone else's dog.
- Ask someone on the street a random question.
- Rate passers-by. Secretly award them marks out of ten as you go along, thinking up expert criticism over their clothing, hairstyle, and footwear choices.
- Create or imagine a life for people you observe in public. Where do they live? Who do they live with? What is their biggest secret? What is in their bag? Where are they going and what will they do when they get there?
- Try to sound Welsh. The key to sounding Welsh is to make sure that your voice goes up at the end of the sentence, so that everything sounds like a question. Don't pronounce the "h" at the beginning of any word or the "r" in the middle of a word.
- Stare at the back of someone's head until they turn around. Or, if you want to be more ambitious, walk close behind someone until they turn around.
- Go for a walk in the woods, around the water, or in your neighborhood.
- Join an organized sports team (adult dodgeball anyone? water polo?).
- Learn a new instrument, or if you already play an instrument, learn a new song. You can learn by watching YouTube videos.
- Learn anything online! Interested in French? Plumbing? How to knit your dog a sweater? How to play a ukulele? There's a YouTube

- video for that!
- Get a psychic reading.
- Have a scavenger hunt. Maybe even organize one and invite people.
- Create your own signature drink or dessert.
- Check your newspaper for cheap thrills, like community concerts, films, and festivals.

Stay in the moment. But when you can, document the fun and share it with others. This will give you a way to remember the fun and let others share in the smile it generates.

Make up words and start using them in conversation. How many adults will have the courage to admit they do not know what your new word means? (See Bernie DeKoven's The Lexifunicon at http://www.deepfun.com/the-lexifunicon/)

Partner Play

Whether you are in a new relationship or have been with the same person for decades, having a habit of being playful can strengthen any relationship.

- Get dressed up for a staying-in date.
- Play follow the leader.
- Catch a midnight movie at the drive-in.
- Write a love letter, the kind you put in the mail. Even if you live together.
- Play strip poker.
- Visit a local toy store.
- Visit a local "toy" store.
- Narrate a silent movie.

- Ask questions from the "relationship closeness induction task" (Google it).
- Play 21 questions.
- Play charades.
- Play the Newlywed Game.
- Participate in an online trivia competition—or other game—and challenge your partner to beat your score. Or collaborate and beat others' scores.
- Keep a relationship journal that you pass back and forth with memories, messages, questions, or sentiments for one another.
- Play video games when the kids are in bed!
- Read a bedtime story.
- Slow dance in the dark.
- Make a meal together.
- Volunteer together.
- Have a picnic.
- Stay at a hotel for the night, and enjoy room service.
- Have sex in a new position or a new place.
- Make "plans" to randomly meet as strangers somewhere in public.
- Wrestle.
- Eat on the good china by candlelight.
- Do a normal activity in an unusual place (get creative).

Child's Play

Children need time to play alone and with other children, but they also love playing with the adults in their lives. Here are some helpful tips to encourage play:

- Play every day! Even if is just for 10 to 15 minutes before dinner. Make it a habit (see Chapter 5).
- Play their way. You know your play type (see Chapter 4), but sometimes it's more of an adventure to play according to someone else's play personality. Or mush them together! An artistic adventure? A performance that involves physical stunts? Writing

- about traveling to another planet?
- Video games are familiar and a great activity where your child can be the expert. Let them teach you how to build a fort in Minecraft or throw a pig in Angry Birds.
- Build a fort in the living room. But, please, don't throw any pigs.
- Make time for screen-free play to engage the imagination and body. Seriously, put it on your calendar.
- Make an old game new by creating new rules or take two games and combine them into a new one.
- Play outdoors. Throw balls. Push kids on swings. Make mud pies. Go on a hike around the neighborhood. Take a nature walk in your backyard.
- Play card games, board games, and silly and wacky kids' games.
- Build a jigsaw puzzle as a family.
- Bake cookies.
- Paint a picture. Or, better yet, paint a wall! You can always cover it later.
- Listen to music together. Sing along. Play rhythm instruments along with music. Have an impromptu dance party!
- Make up song lyrics together.
- Read a book together. Ask questions. Ask them to change the story or make up a new one.
- Play kid games like Follow the Leader, Guess What I Am? I Spy, or Hide and Seek.
- Allow some rough-and-tumble play, within reason. Yep, pig pile on dad!
- Make up a story together, taking turns adding to the story. Make it as outrageous, scary, or funny as you can.
- Go to a science museum, aquarium, or living history museum.
- Try a new restaurant (unless your kid is a super picky eater—in which case, do NOT do this).
- Go to the local music store and let them play an instrument or two.
- Make a video. Let your child write the script, direct, act, and shoot the video. Let go and let them be in charge.

- Create a book together, whether it's a simple project on folded paper or something more elaborate.
- Turn any activity into a party! (thank you Sara Kesty)
- Create your own holiday.
- Celebrate an "unbirthday."
- Make a puzzle by cutting up a picture.
- Create a collage from anything—pictures, trash, paper clips, sticky notes, you name it.
- Play laser tag.
- Camp out in a tent in your own backyard.

Most of all, don't be bossy! Let your children take the lead. Become part of their game rather than trying to dictate the play. Let your child call the shots, make the rules, and determine the pace of play. Ask questions and follow along—you'll likely get drawn into imaginative new worlds that are fun for you, too.

Remember the definition of play includes that it is purposeless, voluntary, and intrinsically motivated. Players have diminished self-consciousness. It's fun and you want to keep doing it! This applies to all players. Playing with your child is not "play" unless you are both having fun.

Snap! The Job's a Game!

Clean out the email inbox: The Email Game (http://emailga.me/) prompts you to make a decision about what to do with each email and gives you a default three minutes if you choose to send a response. You get points for making decisions quickly, see your time, and get a community ranking.

Play Soduku or complete the crossword puzzle in the paper. (You can do this as a group activity by leaving it on the break room table.)

Finding contests in everyday events can transform trying events. The contest can be obvious and the contestants can knowingly participate, or you can have a contest in your head, such as "who will say the word "underwear" first?"

You can also have a fun competition against a timer, another person or against yourself.

Make it cooperative. In CrossFit we partner up to do a challenge. During the class we encourage our partners and race the clock. Ultimately, we want to be the fastest team, but really we are all there for each other.

Do something new. Your brain's hippocampus releases a shot of dopamine in response to novelty. This process also appears to lock in memory, as it engages the amygdala where the brain processes emotional information.

I read about a company called Dopamine (http://dopa.mn/). It bills itself as "a creative agency focused on fun, innovative, gamified campaigns for employees and consumers." I wonder if there are any ADHD kids there? Most likely.

- Share the joke. A friend of mine has a make believe world comprised of all her workmates and their individual quirks. She makes comments on these in private text messages and emails to her daughter, creating outrageous scenarios and making outlandish observations and hypothetical explanations for their behavior.
- Use office products to make a desktop sculpture (Google this).
- Do origami with sticky notes, dollar bills, or other paper (yep, Google it).
- Dress up. Wear something that you normally save for a big date, vacation, or some other "special" occasion: your favorite or lucky underwear, a hat, a tiara, a fancy dress, that outrageous purple eye shadow, or sparkly nail polish.
- Give yourself a new title. Instead of CEO or Founder of PlayDHD, I call myself the Pubah of Play. Get business cards made up to reflect your new title.

- Keep a camera or sketch pad on hand to capture an image or create a work of art.
- Joke with coworkers during coffee breaks
- Have fun at lunch by shooting hoops, playing cards, or completing word puzzles together.
- Make a funny face in the bathroom mirror before getting back to work.
- Keep kids' toys at your desk.
- Dance to some music like no one is watching (if you are in an open office, someone IS watching, so just move your feet and swivel your chair!).
- Make plans with co-workers to go out after work and bowl, play miniature golf, or sing karaoke.
- Have a walking meeting.
- Decorate a white board or chalkboard or the sidewalk or driveway. (At the co-working space where I sometimes play, I took some patterned duct tape and made a hopscotch board on the floor.)
- Post something ridiculous on social media and see what kind of responses you get!
- Practice writing with your non-dominant hand. Not only does this engage your brain, it can help you build a new skill that might come in handy if your dominant hand is ever incapacitated (been there, done that!).

Office game: The Invisible Electric Fence

Draw an invisible line from one point to the other in your office. Try to choose a fairly high-traffic area, preferably near the bathroom or printer for maximum enjoyment. It is then up to you (and your closest co-workers) to avoid crossing the invisible line. You can duck beneath it, or even jump over it, but your aim is to never touch it. The more people that join in, the better the game. Should anyone forget or unknowingly cross your line, all participating players should let out audible gasps of pain.

Stealth Play

In a boring meeting? You may have to amuse yourself silently. Here are some suggestions:

- Pick a random word or phrase and count how many times it is spoken. Without using the word or phrase, can you make a comment or ask a question that might incite someone to use your secret word?
- Rephrase sentences you hear so they sound like Dr. Seuss rhymes. Alternatively, you can create a haiku describing the subject matter of the meeting or your predicament.
- Observe co-worker's behavior for oddities in their speech, body language, habits.
- Make a portrait of the speaker. It looks like you are intently taking notes. Just make sure to take your work of art with you unless you have produced a flattering rendering of the subject.
- Pen twiddling. Can you roll your pen through your fingers in both directions or make it spin in your hand like a helicopter? Practice!
- Combine note-taking with doodling (check out The Sketchnote Handbook by Mike Rodhe).
- Think up an intelligent question to ask. Then, if you space out later, you participated first.
- Guess who will object to or criticize the proposal and on what grounds.
- Wiggle your feet to get the blood flowing.
- Pull your cell phone or pager out of your pocket, glance at it with a startled look, and leave. Obvious, but effective!
- Bring a fidget toy to meetings.
- Do a crossword puzzle. If someone looks over your shoulder and sees the crosswords, whisper that you're stumped on a clue and ask for help.

Let's just skip to the part where I tell you "there's an app for that." There are a gazillion online resources you can search for iApps and strategies to gamify various aspects of work such as personal productivity, task management, and time management.

One of my favorite "time management" apps is called Forest. It is premised on the idea that if you are on your cell phone you are not being productive. You "plant a tree" when you want to be productive. The tree grows for 30 minutes, unless you pick up your phone during that time. In which case the tree dies. The more you "work" the faster you can grow your own forest. I think this is a great idea for managing social interactions as well. Going to dinner—can you grow a tree and stay off your phone and present in conversation for 30 minutes? Play with your kids for 30 minutes, and grow a tree at the same time!

And, if worst comes to worst, there is always doodling, Zentangle, mazes, and online games. My editor said she had to look up "Zentangle." Jeez, I thought everyone knew what this was! But if she doesn't know, perhaps a few of you don't either. Zentangle is essentially an easy-to-learn, relaxing, and fun drawing process in which you use repetitive patterns, deliberate strokes, and your own creativity to create free-flowing images. This is said to improve focus, relaxation and involves many elements of play. I suggest you go to www.zentangle.com. Don't let the images on the site intimidate you. They truly are simple and, most importantly, Zentangle can help make a boring meeting a bit more productive.

CHAPTER 9
ALWAYS END WITH AN ACTION PLAN

If you are like many people with ADHD, you may be reading this first. Because all the good stuff is at the end. It's where the summary is, right? So here is my summary.

- Play is fun.
- Play can lead to higher levels of productivity and happiness—so play is a good thing
- ADHD typically causes challenges of motivation and attention, which can be overcome through play.
- There is science to back up the fact that play especially helps people with ADHD (chapter 2).
- When you were a kid, the adults in your life may have been wrong when they told you to "stop goofing around and get back to work." You might have worked better and harder if you were having fun. Now that you are an adult, that message is still wrong!
- Play is mostly about mindset. Anything can be fun if you think about it the right way.
- Knowing your play personality can help guide your fun (see Chapter 4).
- Throughout history, people with symptoms of ADHD have been considered to be playful and fun. Some of them even have famous quotes about play attributed to them.
- There are some interesting anecdotes, facts, and ideas throughout PlayDHD. Finding them can increase your playfulness.

I wrote PlayDHD to share my discovery that being playful in your thoughts and actions can have a significant impact on managing challenges with ADHD in all areas of your life. As adults, the innate tendency to engage in play has been replaced with the idea that we have to "work hard to get ahead in life." And we mistakenly have accepted that work and play are in opposition. While this is detrimental to the average person, to someone with ADHD it can lead to frustration, depression, anxiety, rebellion, underachievement, and other problems. Play is our natural state of being. It is the context in which our brain functions optimally. We can be play and be productive.

If a specialist told you, "Take this pill every morning and your ADHD symptoms will improve," you would set your intention (and maybe an alarm) and make that a daily habit. In fact, many of us have done just this! As a doctor (yes, I'm playing the doctor card), I am telling you that making it a habit to incorporate more play into your life will improve your symptoms of ADHD. Re-learning how to be playful and have fun starts with setting an intention and having one playful thought or action. It's not as easy as taking a pill, but it's less expensive, has fewer side effects, and can be shared (legally!). The long-term effects of being more playful include better mental and physical health, adaptability, social connections, productivity—and, of course, fun! No pill I've ever taken can make those claims.

I hope that many of the ideas in this book resonate with you. More than that, I hope that you have a concrete plan to implement some of them, or some of your own playful ideas. Think of what you're going to do, where, and with whom. (Colonel Mustard in the dining room with the rope? Just kidding.) The thought of having more potential playmates in my ADHD tribe to have fun with makes me giggle.

While this is a self-help book, hopefully your playfulness will inspire others to take a more playful approach to work and life, making PlayDHD something that indirectly has an impact on a lot of other people in the world.

Like many people with ADHD, I have difficulty with completing things. I was notorious as a kid for leaving one dish in the sink when I had to do dishes. As an adult, I have a bazillion projects started and put aside because something else seemed more interesting and fun. Finishing things (other than an ice cream sundae) is not my forte. But finishing this book is just a start for me. There is much playing to be done!

On your mark, get set…. **PLAY!**

SOURCES

"ADHD: The Entrepreneur's Superpower," Forbes, May 14, 2015.

"ADHD in the Workplace," D Magazine, July/August 2011.

Barkley, Russell A. 2010. Taking Charge of Adult ADHD. New York: The Guilford Press.

Barkley, Russell A., Kevin R. Murphy, and Mariellen Fischer. (2008). ADHD in Adults: What the Science Says. New York: Guilford. p. 7. (University of Massachusetts study.)

Bjorkland, David F., and Anthony D. Pellegrini. 2000. "Child Development and Evolutionary Psychology." Child Development 71: 1687–1708.

Bregman, Peter. "Consider Not Setting Goals in 2013." Harvard Business Review, December 12, 2012.

Brown, Stuart and Christopher Vaughan. 2009. Play: How It Shapes the Brain, Opens the Imagination, and Invigorates the Soul. New York: Avery.

Centers for Disease Control and Prevention (CDC), Key Findings: Trends in the Parent-Report of Health Care Provider-Diagnosis and Medication Treatment for ADHD: United States, 2003–2011. Data from the National Survey of Children's Health (NSCH) 2003 to 2011.

Christie, James F., and E.P. Johnsen. 1983. "The Role of Play in Social-Intellectual Development." Review of Educational Research 53, 93–115.

Csikszentmihalyi, Mihaly. 1990. Flow: The Psychology of Optimal

Experience. New York: Harper & Row.

De Koven, Bernard. 2014. The Playful Path. Copyright by Bernard De Koven and ETC Press.

Dickinson, David K., and Patton O. Tabors, eds. 2001. Beginning Literacy with Language: Young Children Learning at Home and School. Baltimore: Paul Brookes Publishing.

Dr. Sergio Pellis bio on the University of Lethbridge site: http://www.uleth.ca/research-services/research_profiles/dr-sergio-pellis

Duhigg, Charles. 2012. The Power of Habit: Why We Do What We Do in Life and Business. Random House Publishing Group.

Dweck, Carol S. 2006. Mindset: The New Psychology of Success. New York: Random House.

Fisher, Edward P. 1992. "The Impact of Play on Development: A Meta-Analysis." Play and Culture 5(2), 159–181.

Frost, Joe L. 1992. Play and Playscapes. Albany, N.Y.: Delmar.

Gasper, Karen, and Brianna L. Middlewood. May 2014. "Approaching Novel Thoughts: Understanding Why Elation and Boredom Promote Associative Thought More than Distress and Relaxation." Journal of Experimental Social Psychology 52 (pp. 50–57).

Gordon, N.S., S. Burke, H. Akil, S.J. Watson, and J. Panksepp. April 24, 2003. "Socially Induced Brain 'Fertilization': Play Promotes Brain Derived Neurotrophic Factor Transcription in the Amygdala and Dorsolateral Frontal Cortex in Juvenile Rats." Neuroscience Letters 341(1): 17–20.

Greenough, William T., and James E. Black. 1992. "Induction of Brain Structure by Experience: Substrates for Cognitive Development." In Gunnar, M.R., and C.A. Nelson (eds.), Minnesota Symposia on Child Psychology: Developmental Neuroscience, Vol 24 (155–200). Hillside, N.J.: Lawrence A. Erlbaum Associates.

Huber, Reto, Giulio Tononi, and Chiara Cirelli. 2007. "Exploratory Behavior, Cortical BDNF Expression, and Sleep Homeostasis." Sleep 30(2):129–39.

Isenberg, Joan and Nancy L. Quisenberry. "Play a Necessity for All Children." Association for Childhood Education International, January 1, 1988.

Kelly, Kate, and Peggy Ramundo. 2006. You Mean I'm Not Lazy, Stupid or Crazy?! The Classic Self-Help Book with Attention Deficit Disorder. New York: Scribner. 2014.

Kierkegaard, Søren. Either/Or, Swenson 1944; 1959.

Lewis, Vicky, Jill Boucher, Laura Lupton, and Samantha Watson. 2000. "Relationships Between Symbolic Play, Functional Play, Verbal and Non-Verbal Ability in Young Children." International Journal of Language & Communication Disorders 35(1):117–27.

Mann, Sandi, and Rebekah Cadman. 2014. "Does Being Bored Make Us More Creative?" Creativity Research Journal 26(2).

National Institute for Play, "The Promise of Play" (video 5 of 12): https://www.youtube.com/watch?v=nEE1t3mTQoE

Ordonez, Lisa D., Maurice E. Schwietzer, Adam D. Galinsky, and Max H. Bazerman. 2009. "Goals Gone Wild: The Systematic Side Effects of Over-Prescribing Goal Setting." Harvard Business School Working Paper 09-083.

Pansepp, J., J. Burgdorf, C. Turner, and N. Gordon. June 2003. "Modeling ADHD-Type Arousal with Unilateral Frontal Cortex Damage in Rats and Beneficial Effects of Play Therapy." Brain Cognition 52(1):97–105.

Pellegrini, Anthony D., and Robyn M. Holmes. 2006. "The Role of Recess in Primary School." In D. Singer, R. Golinkoff, and K. Hirsh-Pasek (eds.), Play=learning: How Play Motivates and Enhances Children's Cognitive and Socio-Emotional Growth. New York: Oxford University Press.

Pepler, Debra J., and Hildy S. Ross. 1981. "The Effects of Play on Convergent and Divergent Problem Solving." Child Development 52(4): 1202–10.

Pink, Daniel H. 2011. Drive: The Surprising Truth About What Motivates Us. New York: Riverhead Books.

"Staggering New Statistics About ADHD," ADDitude, October 11, 2011.

Stevenson, Harold W., et al. 1990. "Contexts of Achievement: A Study of American, Chinese, and Japanese Children," Monographs of the Society for Research in Child Development 55(1/2): 1–123.

Suomi, S.J. and Harlow, H.F. 1971. "Monkeys Without Play." In Bruner, J.S., Jolly, A., and Sylva, K., eds. 1976. Play: Its Role in Development and Evolution. New York: Basic Books.

Sutton-Smith, Brian. 2009. The Ambiguity of Play. Cambridge, MA: Harvard University Press.

Vygotsky, L.S. 1987. "Thinking and Speech." In R.W. Rieber & A.S. Carton, eds.., The Collected Works of L.S. Vygotsky, Volume 1: Problems of General Psychology (pp. 39–285). New York: Plenum

Press. (Original work published 1934.)

Wolfgang, Charles H, Laura Stannard, and Ithel Jones. (2001). "Block Play Performance Among Preschoolers as a Predictor of Later School Achievement in Mathematics." Journal of Research in Childhood Education 15(2): 173–80.

Wyver, Shirley R., and Susan H. Spence. 1999. "Play and Divergent Problem Solving: Evidence Supporting a Reciprocal Relationship." Early Education and Development 10(4): 419–44

HISTORY OF PLAY SOURCES

1. Neanderthal Man (from: http://www.simplyadhd.co.uk/2009/06/neanderthals-were-peaceful-ones-what-if.html)

2 From: http://www.stuff.co.nz/life-style/parenting/big-kids/five-to-ten/health-nutrition/8996336/Introducing-Attention-Deficit-Hyperactivity-Disorder)

3. From: http://www.mpg.de/617258/pressRelease20100430)

4. Nomad (from: http://www.slate.com/articles/health_and_science/human_nature/2008/06/new_world_disorder.html)

5. Craig Venter: "Creating life in a lab using DNA". The Daily Telegraph - October 16, 2007.

6. From: http://www.additudemag.com/adhd/article/754.html)

Some icon Illustrations by the following artists of the Noun Project: Luke Keil, Christy Presler, Parkjisun, Alex Valdivia, Jon, Michael Wohlwend, Simon Child, Pavel N., Aha-Soft, Ralf Schmitzer, João Proença & freepik.com.

Appomattox Regional Library System
Hopewell, Virginia 23860
01/17